Praise for *Making the Movement: How Ac
Rights with Buttons, Flyers, Pins, and Posters*

"*Making the Movement* compiles over 150 years of the material artifacts
of the most consequential democratic movement in our nation's history,
the long movement for civil rights. The story of Reconstruction, the rise of
Jim Crow and racial terror, key figures and organizations, court decisions,
legislative actions, and the power of grassroots mobilization are all revealed
in the material culture so ably contextualized in this volume. *Making the
Movemen*t is an important scholarly contribution, but many of us will simply
want to have it in our private collections as an indispensable resource to
understanding the Civil Rights Movement, with its material culture and
David Crane as our guides."
**—Brian M. Harward, Professor and Robert G. Seddig Chair in Political
Science, Allegheny College**

"*Making the Movement* describes the indispensable tools—buttons, flyers,
pins and posters— that were used to advance the struggle for human and civil
rights. Flyers were the primary instrument of mass communications. They
recruited people for the sit-ins, informed communities for voter registration
drives, and calls for mass demonstrations. Button and pins were used by those
engaged in the 1960s Civil Rights Movement to show their commitment
to the cause of freedom. Posters were primarily used to engage the American
public and raise funds to support various civil rights organizations."
—Courtland Cox, SNCC Veteran Chair, SNCC Legacy Project

"The Robert H. Jackson Center was the beneficiary of the 2013 world
premiere of David L. Crane's absorbing and poignant exhibit, *Making the
Movement: Civil Rights Museum*. We saw firsthand the impact it had on
Supreme Court Chief Justice John Roberts and Dr. Julian Bond. Now, we are
thrilled this unique project, more timely than ever, can be shared worldwide
through Mr. Crane's new book. This is new and insightful ground."
**—Gregory L. Peterson, cofounder and former director, Robert H. Jackson
Center, Jamestown, New York**

MAKING the MOVEMENT

MAKING the MOVEMENT

How Activists Fought
for Civil Rights
with Buttons, Flyers,
Pins, and Posters

DAVID L. CRANE

Essay by **SILAS MUNRO**

PRINCETON ARCHITECTURAL PRESS · NEW YORK

Making the Movement *is dedicated to the foot soldiers
of the Civil Rights Movement. These men, women,
and children used nonviolent weapons to combat Jim Crow,
and because of their brave actions, we all continue to benefit
from the world they helped create.*

Contents

I Sell the Shadow to Support the Substance.
SOJOURNER TRUTH.

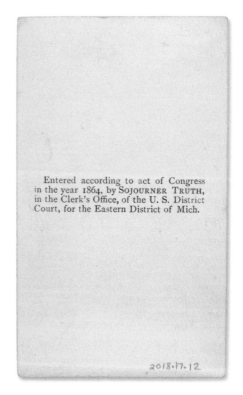

Entered according to act of Congress in the year 1864, by SOJOURNER TRUTH, in the Clerk's Office, of the U. S. District Court, for the Eastern District of Mich.

SILAS MUNRO

Bearing Witness: Call and Response for Civil Rights through Graphic Design

"You're bearing witness helplessly to something which everybody knows, and nobody wants to face."

—James Baldwin, 1962

The protest graphics in *Making the Movement* are the products of a specific kind of urgency. This vital energy does not serve the time-pressured needs of a brand message or the clarion call of capitalism for design to grease the wheels of our economic engines. The buttons, pamphlets, flyers, and posters in this volume, from multiple generations in the Civil Rights struggle, are fury made visible. Across time and space, the objects in this volume capture a series of calls and responses of the dire needs of Black communities in pain, networks of human beings fighting for civil rights who have faced and continue to face oppression. Each material artifact shown speaks to the demands of activists making designs in matters of life and death.

OPPOSITE
Carte de visite portrait of Sojourner Truth, 4.13 × 2.5", 1864

Call-and-response is a musical structure that is made up of two phrases that form a rhythmic dialogue. This pattern of musical refrain begins with an initiator who makes a "call." That opening phrase can be sung, played, or danced, or it can be a medley of all three, and it is always answered by a reciprocal expressive response. Call-and-response as a musical structure has its origins in African music—though you also find it in African American gospel and rhythm and blues, Colombian cumbia, and Peruvian huachihualo forms. This multiplicity of geographies and diasporas was created by the forced migration of Africans through the transatlantic slave trade. The resulting musical aesthetics highlight improvisation and collaboration—skills necessary for community cohesion as conquests by colonial empires stretched across the Americas.

This embedded racial capital in the movement of people also became embedded in typography as a form of "print as property" when, for instance, nineteenth-century enslaved Black printers under duress typeset broadsides that enforced slave catcher laws. Remarkably, the growing Abolitionist movement upset this dynamic as both white and freed Black printers usurped the iconic bold Victorian typographic language, seizing the means of production to print and post messages of emancipation and freedom.[1] An 1864 Emancipation-era carte de visite by Sojourner Truth is inscribed with the words "I Sell the Shadow to Support the Substance."

This poetic statement foreshadows the sacrifices of abolitionists, organizers, and everyday people who used graphic design to demand their equality. In the case of Truth—an innovative, often overlooked contemporary to Frederick Douglass who had been born into slavery and illiteracy—her photographic likeness, printed on cards with liberatory text, funded her life as a traveling preacher, blues singer, and free Black woman.[2] Though they had their differences, Douglass and Truth were pioneers who used both word and image in dynamic ways to further the goals of emancipation.

One of Douglass's key phrases was "the color line," an imaginary barrier between the formerly enslaved people and the former enslavers drawn using the arbitrary rationale of skin color. It would be W. E. B. Du Bois who would take that phrase and construct a life's work that paralleled several critical phases of activism and graphic production reflected in *Making the Movement*'s robust collection.

Du Bois, as a researcher, sociologist, and historian, shrewdly employed graphic design to advocate for African American equality. Much can be delved into with the innovative data visualizations in his 1899 Philadelphia Negro and 1900 Georgia Negro projects.[3] Du Bois also helped start the Civil Rights movements as a cofounder of the National Association for the Advancement of Colored People (NAACP). He served as the first editor of *The Crisis*, the official publication of the NAACP, which is still in production today. The NAACP's graphic output appears throughout this volume, and *The Crisis* represents a visual and intellectual engine of that output. Reflecting in 1951 on the impact of the enduring publication, its business manager, George Schuyler, recalled, "Here for the first time with brilliance, militancy, facts, photographs and persuasiveness, a well-edited magazine challenged the whole concept of white supremacy then nationally accepted."[4] Du Bois commissioned a stirring array of designers, artists, and writers during his tenure as editor, including seminal figures who emerged out of the Harlem Renaissance: Aaron Douglas, Frank Walts, and Louise E. Jefferson.

Jefferson was a prolific maker: a graphic designer, calligrapher, cartographer, and photographer. *Opportunity* magazine, another significant publication of the Harlem Renaissance, also featured her work on its covers. Over Jefferson's long life she photographed iconic figures in Black culture and protest, including Martin Luther King Jr.[5]

We can see King's image, touch his fingerprints, and feel his essence as another strong voice in the turning tide on social justice. There is no other graphic symbol that speaks to the

Louise R. Latimer (cover designer), W. E. B. Du Bois (editor), *The Crisis* 13, no. 5 (March 1917), letterpress, 9.75 × 6.88"

XI

TOP
Anonymous designer for the American Federation of State, County, and Municipal Employees (AFSCME), *I Am a Man,* **letterpress, 14 x 21.5", 1968**
BOTTOM
Based on a design by Josiah Wedgwood, "Am I not a man and a brother?" woodcut appearing on the broadside publication of John Greenleaf Whittier's "Our Countrymen in Chains," 10.5 x 9", 1837

culmination of his legacy, expressed in his last speech on the eve of his assassination recounting his journey "to the mountaintop," than the 1968 poster *I AM A MAN*. The poster's proclamation is typeset in bold letterpress with a simple but profound statement that asks not to be seen only as a Black person, but as a human being who is deserving of equal treatment. The signs were produced by the Memphis sanitation workers' union to protest the negligent deaths of two Black sanitation workers. King took trips to Memphis several times that spring to support the workers' movement. The poster is composed with a straightforward and minimalist power that matches the insistence of its message. The underline beneath "AM" is a form of visual punctuation—it is a response to the call of nineteenth-century abolitionists: "Am I not a man and a brother?"

The phrase echoes a woodcut of an enchained enslaved African that accompanied the broadside poster publication of John Greenleaf Whittier's antislavery poem "Our Countrymen in Chains." The broadsheet design is itself an iteration of a seal designed by Josiah Wedgwood for the Society for the Abolition of Slavery in England. The phrase "Am I not a man and a brother?" and the image of a Black man in chains also appeared on nineteenth-century abolitionists' lapel pins—early precursors to the pins and buttons that appear throughout the following chapters.[6]

The empowerment found in the refrain "I AM A MAN" was mirrored in calls for "Freedom Now" by the NAACP and its allies, which tragically evolved and increased in urgency as the continued violence against Black bodies through police brutality and the sacrifices of the lives of King and other activists battered the movements. This energy shifted into the Black Power movements of the late 1960s, 1970s, and early 1980s.

In the aftermath of the police and FBI negligence around the murder of civil rights activist Malcolm X in 1966,[7] two young activists, Bobby Seale and Huey P. Newton, launched a groundbreaking movement named the Black Panther Party.

It was first called the Party for Self-Defense, and it encouraged community members to lead armed watches to protect against police violence in Black neighborhoods. Making their rounds, Party members projected a bad and bodacious image in the streets, with the sartorial flair of knit berets, leather jackets, and rifles in tow. The Party began in Oakland but spread its values of anti-racism, human rights for all, and radical socialist philosophy through various social programs and public awareness announcements. The design corner-stone of the party's activist messaging was the *Black Panther,* a weekly newsletter that cost twenty-five cents and achieved a circulation of three hundred thousand copies at its height—competing with the distribution scale of papers in a number of US cities.[8]

During its most active phase from 1968 to 1971, the party expanded nationally to have affiliates in more than fifty cities. The *Black Panther* offered a "Black Community News Service" that highlighted stories of grassroots Black liberation, energized and inspired community action, and served as a printed embodiment of the party's Ten-Point Program—a political, social, and philosophical platform that called for full employment, equitable housing, and access to education and health care.[9]

Black Panther Party principles—which included the anti-capitalist ethos of Karl Marx, the adoption of Second Amend-ment rights by Americans of color, and the use of organizing practices developed by labor unions—were red-flagged by FBI surveillance. The Bureau manipulated the press to stigma-tize the image of the Party in order to justify aggressive actions by FBI agents, which included imprisoning key Panthers such as Huey P. Newton and Angela Davis. They even went as far as assassinating members, as in the case of Chicago chapter chairman Fred Hamilton.[10] FBI harassment also included ongoing pressure to shutter the *Black Panther* newsletter's production. Designer, illustrator, and Minister of Culture for the Party Emory Douglas remembers that lawyers shepherded the newspapers from the printer to safeguard their public distribution.[11]

Today a protest march can be attended as easily from our bedroom as from the streets of our local neighborhood. As technology advances, so do additional spaces for creating and displaying protest graphics. More people attended the protest marches honoring the tragically murdered George Floyd in the summer of 2020 on their phones than in person. One can easily see social media posts as the digital broadsides of our day. Our daily feeds are flooded with digital compositions thanks to the graphic power of personal computers that are now integral to the contemporary design process—whether a formally trained designer is at the helm or not. Protest signs get generated with the minimal friction of a few double taps in the mobile application of your choice.

Digital production has revolutionized the typographic language of protest as much as digital venues have increased the audience of protest graphics. Vocal Type Foundry, founded by the Black graphic and type designer Tré Seals in 2016, is a pioneer of this vanguard. Martin (which is used as the display typeface for this book) is a revival of the design of the Memphis sanitation workers' "I AM A MAN" signs. Martin and other typefaces including Marsha, Carrie, and Ruben represent the painstaking archival research that Seals has contributed to the typographic representation of other protest movements, including the Stonewall uprising, women's suffrage, and the Chicano Moratorium, respectively.

In the typeface Redaction, a collaborative effort by Titus Kaphar, Reginald Dwayne Betts, Forest Young, and Jeremy Mickel, a shifting pixel grid becomes a metaphor for extreme racial discrimination in the US legal system: notably, its cash bail practices and how they disproportionately result in prison time for poor people of color. Redaction is essentially a mix of Times New Roman and Century Schoolbook—both types heavily associated with legal documents. Rather than being sold commercially, Redaction is served up in an Open Font

re dac ti on — a multiplicity of typographic, legal, and human histories

Titus Kaphar and Reginald Dwayne Betts (concept); Forest Young (creative direction); Jeremy Mickel (typeface design), Redaction typeface, 2019

License, which permits the typeface to be free for use as
an open-source tool. This spirit of collaboration and free
exchange is one of the Civil Rights Movement's goals that
has come to fruition.

    With all the cycles of progress and setback, the 1940s
NAACP slogan "Finish the Fight" comes back to mind. Facing
the global forces of the COVID-19 pandemic suggests a new
reality of a metaphoric endemic battle against restrictions
of our collective rights. The calls and responses of solidarity
among protesters in the Civil Rights, women's liberation,
countercultural, LGBTQIA+, and Black Lives Matter movements all set up this current moment of embracing an economy
of means necessary through centuries of making design
under duress. And yet the increased accessibility that comes
in bearing witness to the graphic evidence in *Making the
Movement* leaves us with hope to continue fighting.

Nonviolent Weapons

Making the Movement: How Activists Fought for Civil Rights with Buttons, Flyers, Pins, and Posters is the companion book to Making the Movement: Civil Rights Museum—a traveling exhibition that explores the material culture of the Civil Rights Movement and how those objects helped the Movement achieve its objectives. The museum consists of artifacts such as buttons, flyers, posters, and pinbacks from Emancipation to the twenty-first century. These were not collector's items when they were produced; they were the nonviolent weapons used by those in the Movement to combat racial discrimination and violence.

From the days of Reconstruction, after the Civil War, through the rise of Jim Crow and the fight against disenfranchisement and segregation, the material culture of the Movement was integral to its changing goals and tactics. Each generation faced unique challenges, but one constant was the use of material culture to meet those challenges. Wearing, displaying, or holding these objects made the Movement

"Making the Movement"
button, 1.25", 2015

possible: they helped raise money, recruit members, inform the public, influence legislation, change minds, and create a shared sense of belonging to a growing movement.

I purchased my first artifact from the Civil Rights Movement fifty years after it was made. It is a small, faded blue pinback with the words "Member NAACP 1954." As I held it in my hand, I realized that funds generated by the sale of that, and earlier National Association for the Advancement of Colored People membership pinbacks, had helped the NAACP Legal Defense and Education Fund to bring a class-action lawsuit against the Board of Education of Topeka, Kansas—which led to the landmark 1954 *Brown v. Board of Education of Topeka* Supreme Court decision declaring segregation in public education unconstitutional. I began to understand that this and similar objects told the history of the Civil Rights Movement. These were not merely souvenirs or memorabilia; they were the tools those in the Movement used to achieve their objectives of ending segregation, disenfranchisement, violence, and poverty, and they reflected their evolving strategies to accomplish those goals. Material culture helped to spread the word about sit-ins and boycotts, organize marches, raise funds, grow support for legislation, and elect candidates that supported civil rights.

After several years of collecting, I created a museum exhibition with the goal of preserving these objects. *Making the Movement* debuted at the Robert H. Jackson Center in Jamestown, New York, in 2013. The exhibition has since traveled to a wide range of institutions such as Elon University in North Carolina and the Community Folk Art Center in Syracuse, New York.

While *Making the Movement* was at Allegheny College in Meadville, Pennsylvania, in November 2013, Dr. Julian Bond toured the exhibition as part of a retrospective on the fiftieth anniversary of the Civil Rights Act of 1964.

ABOVE
NAACP Member pinback, .75", 1954

As chairman emeritus of the NAACP, Bond was particularly interested in their pinback buttons. He saw, firsthand, the impact these objects had on the Movement, and realized how they helped make it possible.

Six months later, in May 2014, I had the privilege of spending a week with Dr. Bond, touring sites significant to the Civil Rights Movement throughout the South, including, in Alabama, the Sixteenth Street Baptist Church in Birmingham, the Rosa Parks Museum in Montgomery, and the Edmund Pettus Bridge in Selma. While we toured the Martin Luther King, Jr. National Historical Park in Atlanta, Georgia, I wore a button from the March on Washington for Jobs and Freedom, and I asked Dr. Bond about the impact of material culture. He initially stated that the NAACP gave away the "Member" pinbacks, but as soon as he said it, he corrected himself. "No. No. No. We sold them. We used that money!" His insight helped me understand how integral these objects were to achieving the Movement's varied objectives.

While eating at Paschal's in Atlanta with Dr. Bond, I met former ambassador Andrew Young, executive director of the Southern Christian Leadership Conference, and John Lewis, US representative for Georgia's Fifth Congressional District. I interviewed Congressman Lewis in June 2014 and asked whether he was aware of the material culture while he participated in the Civil Rights Movement. "Not at first," he said. He recalled his involvement in the Nashville sit-ins in February through May 1960 but did not remember seeing any buttons or posters. He said that he was young (twenty) and inexperienced, and that he may not have noticed them. But he recalled how the material culture of the Movement was "everywhere" by the time he was the youngest speaker at the March on Washington for Jobs and Freedom three years later, in 1963. It was inspirational to hear from leaders of the Civil Rights Movement that material culture was an integral part of the Movement—even if those activists had been largely unaware of their significance at the time.

This book is organized chronologically into five chapters. These chapters, which represent five different eras, are designed to show that as the Civil Rights Movement's objectives and tactics changed, the use of material culture remained a constant. These objects helped achieve the objectives of the Civil Rights Movement, and retrospectively, the artifacts in *Making the Movement* help us understand that struggle in a deeper way. They bore silent witness to the fight against Jim Crow, and now they can speak to future generations to provide powerful lessons that organized resistance to racism can be successful. Whether it is the legalist approach advocated by W. E. B. Du Bois, the peaceful protest advocated by Rev. Dr. Martin Luther King Jr., or the armed self-defense advocated by the Black Panthers, the physical object will always play a role in these strategies.

Chapter One, "Separate and Unequal (1863–1938)," begins with the first material culture of the Civil Rights Movement after Reconstruction through the early twentieth century. It demonstrates how the objects produced were a way to pursue the goal of outlawing Jim Crow practices. The formation in 1910 of the NAACP marked the beginning of the modern Civil Rights Movement in the twentieth century. The NAACP and other civil rights organizations used objects such as pinbacks, posters, and pamphlets to raise money, recruit new members, and launch campaigns such as the anti-lynching crusade in the 1920s and 1930s.

Chapter Two, "Finish the Fight (1939–1950)," explores the Movement during World War II. Many civil rights organizations initially opposed the entry of the United States into the Second World War and stressed that their focus was on problems on the home front. The NAACP's position reflected an isolationist sentiment in the United States and argued that equality and jobs should be at the center of their legislative agenda. Once the United States went to war in 1941, civil rights organizations sought to link the participation of African Americans in the war effort to the fight for civil rights at home. The material culture produced by civil rights organizations helped achieve some victories during, and after, the war. For example, the items used by the Double V campaign against fascism and racism, and for the proposed March on Washington, led by A. Philip Randolph, resulted in Executive Order 8802, which outlawed discrimination in the defense industry, and the Fair Employment Practices Committee, which was established to help enforce the order.

Chapter Three, "Segregation and Desegregation (1951–1959)," is about how material culture impacted the fight against segregation in the 1950s. Support for racial equality increased after World War II because of the efforts of the NAACP and other civil rights organizations, as well as the contribution of African Americans to the war effort. Material culture was used to advance the notion that the shared ideals that aided the war effort were the same democratic values Americans should honor to end Jim Crow. A ninefold increase in membership in the NAACP allowed for its Legal Defense and Education Fund to challenge segregation in the courts. Objects such as buttons, pamphlets, and pinbacks were a key part of this strategy. They helped to raise awareness about the negative impacts of segregation, as well as to recruit new members and generate funds. The result of these efforts was the 1954 *Brown v. Board of Education* decision, which declared segregation in public schools unconstitutional and set a precedent for challenging segregation through the courts. *Brown* put the power of the courts on the side of protecting civil rights, and the Movement gained momentum, but desegregation was agonizingly slow and resistance was widespread and frequently violent. The success of the Montgomery bus boycott propelled Rev. Dr. Martin Luther King Jr. as a national leader for civil rights, and material culture continued to be part of the strategy to achieve the Movement's varied objectives.

Chapter Four, "Growing the Movement (1960–1965)," discusses how civil rights organizations worked together in defining the objectives of the Movement in the 1960s. The objects they used helped achieve two of the main objectives of the Civil Rights Movement: federal legislation outlawing both segregation and disenfranchisement. Long-standing organizations such as the Congress of Racial Equality and the Southern Christian Leadership Conference worked with student groups like the Student Nonviolent Coordinating Committee and the Southern Student Organizing Committee. These groups produced objects to organize the sit-ins, the Freedom Rides, and the March on Washington for Jobs and Freedom, as well as Freedom Summer and the Selma marches. King was wearing a button made for the March on Washington during his "I Have a Dream" speech on August 28, 1963. The march showed support for the civil rights bill, and activists used material culture to lobby for its passage. These combined efforts resulted in the Civil Rights Act of 1964, which outlawed discrimination based on race, color, religion, and national origin. The nation's conscience was shocked after the violence in Selma, and material culture helped to press for the passage of the Voting Rights Act of 1965, which provided federal supervision of elections in voting districts with a history of voter suppression.

Chapter Five, "Visions of Freedom (1966–1980s)," looks at how the two pillars of Jim Crow, segregation and disenfranchisement, were outlawed, but debates remained within the Movement over its objectives and the best tactics to achieve those goals. Should the Movement focus on ending racial discrimination, disenfranchisement, and violence, or focus on alleviating poverty and creating jobs? And what was the best way to accomplish those objectives: electoral politics, protest and advocacy, or militant self-defense? King's assassination in 1968 and the unrest that followed complicated these questions and intensified the debate. The objects used in this struggle helped spread these diverse messages and reflected the many visions for the future of the Civil Rights Movement.

After the 1980s, many felt less of a shared sense of a cohesive movement, but that did not mean the struggle was over, or that physical objects played less of a role. Material culture helped those in the Movement confront the challenges faced by previous generations, as well as those that lingered into the twenty-first century, such as poverty, underfunded schools, employment and housing discrimination, mass incarceration, police violence, and voter suppression. Differing visions over goals and tactics were reflected in the material culture produced, and its significance to the Movement continues. The current state of the Movement, and its future, are discussed in the book's afterword.

◆　◆　◆

Many of the objectives of the Civil Rights Movement were accomplished, but the arc that King famously described in his 1965 speech "Remaining Awake Through a Great Revolution" ("the arc of the moral universe is long, but it bends toward justice") is curving backward again toward our dark past. None of the gains made by the effort and sacrifice of countless participants in the Movement are guaranteed to last forever. There are powerful forces mobilizing to roll them back, and one of the lessons of *Making the Movement* is that the arc can change course but it will take effort. Organizing for political, social, and economic change works, but those who fight the battle need help. Material culture provided the tools to help combat Jim Crow, but the hard work continues and success is not guaranteed—no more guaranteed than it was for earlier generations of activists that worked their entire lives for a cause and still never saw significant change occur. I think of activists at the turn of the twentieth century, whose biggest concerns were lynching, forced labor, and a Ku Klux Klan that numbered in the millions. Although there were some successes, they did not live to see many of their goals realized: it took generations of effort to finally bear fruit.

Making the Movement fills a gap in the scholarship of the Civil Rights Movement, as well as that of material culture. Works about the Civil Rights Movement have neglected to focus on the objects that participants used to achieve their objectives, and works about material culture have left out the Civil Rights Movement. For a complete historiography, refer to the *Making the Movement: Civil Rights Museum* website, makingthemovement.com.

The Civil Rights Movement ushered in the most significant social and political changes in the history of the United States. The material culture Americans used reflected the changing goals and tactics of those involved and helped the Movement achieve many of its objectives. Countless activists risked, and lost, their lives in the struggle to get the nation to live up to its own ideals. These objects helped them do it. These buttons, flyers, pamphlets, posters, and pinbacks were the nonviolent weapons of the Civil Rights Movement. Those who forged and wielded them helped make the Movement.

OPPOSITE
Civil Rights Movement leaders Rev. Dr. Martin Luther King Jr. and John Lewis (left) at the March on Washington for Jobs and Freedom, August 28, 1963

CHAPTER ONE

Separate and Unequal (1863–1938)

The struggle for equality in America began at its very inception. The founding documents of the United States made bold promises of equality and liberty, and yet, for many, those sentiments were mere words on a piece of paper. For African Americans, their experience was very different from the dream promised by our nation's forefathers. Centuries of enslavement culminated in a bloody war that almost tore the country apart. After the Civil War, the promise of freedom and equality was extended to millions with the passage of the Thirteenth, Fourteenth, and Fifteenth Amendments to the Constitution. The Thirteenth Amendment (1865) made slavery illegal, the Fourteenth Amendment (1868) guaranteed citizenship and equal protection under the law, and the Fifteenth Amendment (1870) prevented the government from denying someone the vote based on "race, color, or previous condition of servitude." The crime of slavery was gone, and for millions of African Americans, the days they had yearned for seemed at hand [FIGURE 1.1].

OPPOSITE
National Negro Business League Executive Committee (Booker T. Washington seated, second from left), 1910

Emancipation

1.1
Emancipation carte de visite,
2.5 x 4", 1863

The Civil War resulted in the end of slavery in the United States, but after the US Army left the South in 1877, a new era of discrimination, segregation, and violence began. White citizens and government officials constructed a system of racist practices and laws collectively known as Jim Crow, the effects of which persist to this day. From slavery to citizenship in five years seemed like the answer to so many millions of prayers, but the end of those rights in a system of segregation and disenfranchisement was as bitter as freedom was sweet. White supremacist organizations such as the Ku Klux Klan and the White League used violence and intimidation to prevent African Americans from participating in American society, economics, and politics. Resistance to Jim Crow was difficult and dangerous, but African Americans risked their lives for the next hundred years to bring this system to an end.

Organizing for civil rights had begun even before the Civil War, and the number of organizations designed to aid African Americans increased over the course of the nineteenth century. African Americans formed mutual aid societies, lodges, and orders to provide services such as insurance, death benefits, and contributions to funeral expenses that were not available to them due to widespread discrimination. These organizations served a vital role in helping African Americans to navigate the confines of Jim Crow and also provided settings for intellectual debate and camaraderie. As forums for grassroots organizing, they created the foundation of what became known as the Civil Rights Movement.

In the United States, African Americans were refused membership to all-white organizations like literary societies, clubs, churches, lodges, and mutual aid societies such as the International Order of Odd Fellows (IOOF). The IOOF's lodges in the United Kingdom, however, did not have the same limits. In 1842, Peter Ogden, born in Jamaica but a member of Victoria Lodge No. 448 of Liverpool, England, traveled to New York City as a crewman of the *Patrick Henry*. Ogden visited Mother African Methodist Episcopal Zion Church in Harlem, a congregation founded at the turn of the nineteenth century after breaking with the Methodist church, which routinely discriminated against African Americans.[1]

Ogden befriended several members of the Philomathean Society, a literary and debating group formed in 1830 by members of Mother African Methodist Episcopal Zion Church. This society provided an outlet for bright minds to share ideas and strategies about the perils facing their communities, and when Ogden learned that these men were denied a charter by the all-white IOOF, he returned to Liverpool to petition the creation of a charter through his lodge. The Committee of Management of Victoria Lodge No. 448 granted that charter, and a committee of five Grand

Masters and Noble Fathers was created to form a new lodge in New York City known as the Philomathean Lodge No. 646, Grand United Order of Oddfellows (GUOOF).

The committee of Grand Masters, including Peter Ogden, arrived in New York on February 27, 1843, and instituted the Philomathean Lodge's forty-eight members on March 1, 1843. Along with the charter, Ogden also brought from England all the books and paraphernalia to which the lodge was now entitled. These items included instructional manuals and guidebooks explaining Oddfellows procedures as well as the material culture of ribbons, badges, medals, clothing, and signage adopted by American lodges from the English model. These objects were an important part of the success and growth of the GUOOF throughout the United States. They allowed members to recruit others, raise money, promote the ideals of the GUOOF, and create a sense of shared identity.

Ogden became the lodge's first leader and quickly granted dispensations for the creation of more lodges. The Hamilton Lodge was established in New York in 1844, followed by six more across the United States in 1845; by the time of Ogden's death in 1852, there were twenty-five lodges across the East Coast of the United States and Bermuda, totaling 1,470 members. The lodges provided members and their families financial support for disability, sickness, burial, and widowhood, but they were equally concerned with morality and social outreach.

Members were expected to support each other's families and to serve as moral leaders in the community. They took vows to remain "sober, honest, industrious and benevolent, a good husband, a kind father, a loyal and virtuous citizen." By living a virtuous life and abiding by the GUOOF's creed, lodge members demonstrated to their communities, as well as to whites, their ability to prosper in spite of the discrimination faced by African Americans. The GUOOF taught that lodges across the world united mankind—a message that members would have liked the supporters of Jim Crow to receive.

Peter Ogden and the Philomathean Lodge No. 646 enjoyed great success for many years, but his story ended tragically. Ogden fell out of favor with lodge members, and he stopped coming to the lodge altogether. After succumbing to a painful illness, Ogden was buried without receiving the benefits deserving of lodge members, and without any GUOOF honors.

Members of the order in England heard about Ogden's death, as well as a failed attempt he had made to reunite with his sister, and they tried to find her in the United Kingdom. She knew of her brother's disillusionment with the GUOOF and blamed the falling out for his death. After the death one of the order's founders, the organization addressed its prohibition of women at the behest of Ogden's widow. A motion was passed to allow the wife, mother, or daughter of any lodge member to become a contributing member and to enjoy the benefits of membership. Although considered members of the IOOU, women were required to form a separate women's auxiliary organization. Patrick H. Reason, an engraver, lithographer, and abolitionist, led the successful effort to officially associate a female group with the United Order in England, and in September 1858, the Household of Ruth was formed.

The GUOOF, far from being a secret society, held numerous public events and celebrations. In each, the material culture they wore, held, and distributed greatly contributed to the order's recruitment, growth, and fulfillment of its objectives. The organization garnered attention from newspapers such as the *Washington Republican*:

> Yesterday was a gala day for our colored citizens, the occasion being a grand procession of the different lodges of the Grand United Order of Odd Fellows, which visited Washington for the purpose of celebrating the 28th anniversary of the Order, and are holding a convention in Georgetown, at Market House Hall.

1.2
Boaz, Alabama Chapter
of the Household of Ruth
No. 91 Grand United Order
of Oddfellows member
ribbon, 2.25 x 7.5", 1890

The procession also garnered negative attention, which represented the prevailing attitude of whites toward Blacks in the nineteenth century, but membership in the GUOOF steadily grew. After the Civil War, the number of lodges grew to more than one thousand by 1886. By the turn of the twentieth century, the number of lodges had doubled, and membership had leaped from 36,853 to 155,537. Key to this growth was the material culture produced by the GUOOF such as the Household of Ruth ribbon worn by women in their Alabama chapter.[2]

The pin with ribbon in FIGURE 1.2 is typical of the regalia used by lodge members. This ribbon is particularly rare because it is from the Household of Ruth, which had fewer members than the all-male chapters. It features shaking hands—typical imagery for mutual aid societies in the nineteenth century—symbolizing the cooperation necessary for the lodge to fulfill its objectives.

The Knights of Pythias of North America, South America, Europe, Asia, Africa, and Australia (KPNSAEAA) was another mutual aid society that used material culture to achieve its objectives [FIGURE 1.3]. Pythias was a fourth century BCE Greek soldier who practiced a religion founded by the mathematician Pythagoras, who believed a virtuous life was necessary to free the soul. An earlier organization, the Knights of Pythias, had been founded on this principle in 1864 but refused admission to Black members. One of that group's founders, Justus Henry Rathbone, based the society's rituals, constitution, and mission on the Pythian values of "Benevolence, Friendship, and Charity." He also developed the organization's hierarchy, where members worked from page to esquire to knight, with the highest office being supreme chancellor.[3]

These same virtues, mission, and hierarchy were used in the founding of the KPNSAEAA in 1880, but the newer lodge was not merely imitating the all-white Knights of Pythias. While the Knights of Pythias's philosophy was not based on

1.3
Supreme Lodge Knights of Pythias of North America, South America, Europe, Asia, Africa, and Australia Second Lieutenant certificate, 23 x 19", 1919

Judeo-Christian teachings, the "Colored Knights," as they were commonly known, specified belief in the God of Abraham. This distinction became important to recruit new members because of the significant role churches played in African American communities. Churches served not only as houses of worship but also became platforms to discuss the impact of Jim Crow. By 1897, the KPNSAEAA had forty thousand members, with Grand Lodges in twenty states and other lodges in the West Indies and Central America. It distributed $60,000 worth of benefits annually and had a women's auxiliary, typical of most fraternal lodges.[4]

The revenue for this aid came from its members, and its material culture played an important role. Elaborate regalia

Knights of Pythias of North America, South America, Europe, Asia, Africa, and Australia "John Mitchell Jr. for Supreme Chancellor" pinback, 1", 1921
1.5 (LEFT)
Owl's Club Afro-American pinback, .75", 1920s–30s
1.6 (MIDDLE)
"I Am Helping to Build Booker Washington Birthplace" pinback, 1.25", 1930s

was common, but the only required purchase was a Knights of Pythias badge, which cost members seventy-five cents. In addition to funding benefits, the publicly worn badges and other regalia helped in recruiting new members.[5]

As the KPNSAEAA grew in size and influence, it attracted African American business leaders, educators, clergy, and politicians such as John Mitchell Jr., who won the position of supreme chancellor of the Virginia chapter after a long career serving the Black community [FIGURE 1.4]. Mitchell was born July 11, 1863, in Henrico County, Virginia, to parents who were enslaved. In 1884, he became the second editor of the newspaper the *Richmond Planet*, a Black weekly paper founded by formerly enslaved people in 1882. He remained its editor for forty-five years, during which time he used his position and his paper to protest all forms of racial discrimination, especially lynching, earning for himself the title of "the fighting editor." By 1887, the paper was one of the highest circulating Black newspapers in the South. Mitchell served as Jackson Ward's delegate to the Richmond City Council from 1888 to 1896 and ran for governor of Virginia on an all-Black ticket in 1921. Under Mitchell's leadership, the KPNSAEAA continued to provide community services such as insurance, burial services, and other welfare functions not available to African Americans.[6]

Social clubs continued to serve an important function in the twentieth century. The Owl's Whist Club was founded by sixteen African American men on February 14, 1914, in Charleston, South Carolina. The purpose of the club was to provide its members an opportunity to socialize, play cards, and relax. Thousands of similar members-only clubs existed for whites, but due to segregation, African Americans were not permitted to join. Within the confines of Jim Crow, the seemingly simple act of meeting with friends held significant meaning; the club's very existence was a message of defiance, and wearing an "Owl's Club" pinback [FIGURE 1.5] signified one's opposition to it. The "Owls" prided themselves on not charging annual membership dues, so the club funded its expansion by selling items like this pinback. In 1939, after the club's twenty-fifth anniversary, members built a clubhouse referred to as the Roost. The Owl's Whist Club celebrated its hundredth anniversary in 2014.[7]

During the period when KPNSAEAA was founded, Booker T. Washington was the most prominent African American leader in the United States because of his ability to address the many concerns of the Black community while garnering powerful white supporters [FIGURE 1.6]. Born into slavery in 1856, Washington was eager to succeed, and in 1872, he walked five hundred miles from West Virginia to attend Hampton Institute in Virginia. At Hampton,

Washington caught the attention of the school's president, Samuel Chapman Armstrong, who promoted agricultural and industrial education for African Americans.[8]

After graduation, Washington taught at Hampton before being appointed by his mentor, in 1881, to head the Tuskegee Normal School in Alabama. The institute's first classes were held in an AME Zion church, and students built the school on the grounds of a former plantation.[9] Under Washington's leadership, Tuskegee Institute (as it became known) emphasized economic nationalism, race pride, racial solidarity, and interracial goodwill. He argued that economic uplift, especially business development and industrial education, was the best course for Black advancement. He was an ardent self-promoter and understood how material culture could help spread his message, while generating income.

Washington gained state funding for the Institute, as well as the support of wealthy white philanthropists such as Andrew Carnegie and John D. Rockefeller. Most Northern whites supported the status quo and were attracted to Washington's model for education because it promoted individual responsibility within the confines of Jim Crow. Washington garnered much criticism for this approach from other leaders such as W. E. B. Du Bois, but with increasing contributions, Washington continued to expand opportunities for African Americans. He helped pilot a program that created five thousand rural schools for Blacks in the South with the help of Julius Rosenwald, one of the owners of Sears, Roebuck and Company, and in 1900 founded the National Negro Business League (NNBL). Material culture played an important role in establishing the NNBL and continued to do so as the League grew. The NNBL produced pinbacks, which they gave to their thousands of members. This incentive helped bring in funds, recruit new members, and raise awareness about the goals of the organization.[10]

The NNBL was a national network of Black professionals and businessmen that fostered the development of

Black-owned and -operated enterprises. The League helped Washington gain allies throughout the Black business community, churches, higher education, and newspapers. This network of prominent Black men developed into an influential political and economic force that inspired many of its members to advocate for civil rights. One such member was R. H. Boyd.[11]

In 1905, the Tennessee General Assembly passed a law to segregate Nashville's streetcars. Local Black leaders were determined to protest the law through a boycott of the public transportation system. Boyd, then head of the local chapter of the NNBL, led the boycott and established a rival Black-owned public transit system known as the Union Transportation Company (UTC).[12]

Boyd founded the UTC on August 29, 1905, but faced multiple challenges from the start. Due to segregated housing, Black neighborhoods were widely dispersed, and the company had difficulty meeting the demand. The UTC used electric streetcars, so Nashville's city leaders placed a tax on electric streetcars in 1906 in order to weaken the Black-owned

1.7 (LEFT)
**"In Memory of R. H. Boyd"
pinback, .75", 1922**
1.8 (RIGHT)
**National Negro Business
League pinback, .75", 1922**

business. The UTC went out of business within a year, and the boycott was ultimately unsuccessful, but its long duration was one source of inspiration for the bus boycotts of the 1950s. The pinback in FIGURE 1.7 was made following Boyd's death in 1922, and those who wore it kept alive the memory of a man who spent his life in the service of advancing civil rights. Although he did not live to see Nashville's streetcars desegregated, his tactics, and the material culture he inspired, influenced the next generation of activists. The pinback in FIGURE 1.8 was made the same year he died and was worn by the members that carried on his fight.[13]

No other civil rights organization deployed material culture more to its advantage than the National Association for the Advancement of Colored People. The NAACP became the first national organization dedicated solely to the goal of protecting the civil rights of African Americans. Like the African American lodges, fraternal organizations, and mutual aid societies of the early twentieth century, the NAACP produced objects such as pinbacks, badges, ribbons, pamphlets, leaflets, and flyers, and used the sale from these items to fund its activities. Members wore, sold, and distributed them, and membership slowly grew nationwide.[14]

The NAACP arose from the Niagara Movement—a protest organization of Black intellectuals that sought to place Black civil rights on the national agenda. The movement was founded in 1905, when W. E. B. Du Bois and William Monroe Trotter—editor of the *Boston Guardian*—met on the Canadian side of Niagara Falls to discuss their objectives: desegregation, voting rights, and equal opportunity to education. Members of the Niagara Movement believed a concerted legalist effort was the best approach to achieving civil rights, in contrast to the accommodationist approach of Booker T. Washington. Du Bois had initially found much to admire in Washington's emphasis on racial solidarity, self-reliance, and economic advancement, but Du Bois was a far more ardent advocate for Black equality. The differences between the men became more pronounced as disenfranchisement, discrimination, and violence against African Americans intensified during the early twentieth century.[15]

Du Bois insisted on the need for African Americans to pursue a liberal arts education and scientific fields of study. He believed that a "talented tenth" of educated Black leaders could successfully advocate for the rights of all African Americans. Du Bois had trained as a historian and was a pioneer in the emerging field of sociology, so he understood the importance of material culture in advocating for political rights and in demonstrating to the public the achievements of African Americans. He helped create a display for the 1900 Paris World's Fair—the "Exhibit of American Negroes"—that highlighted the achievements of African Americans since Emancipation. By presenting these objects to the public, Du Bois was able "to give, in as systematic and compact form, as possible, the history and present condition of…American Negroes."[16] He drew upon sociological data that he and his students had compiled to demonstrate the progress African Americans had achieved, as well as the tremendous opposition they faced from a hostile white public. The exhibit was awarded a grand prize—four gold medals, five silver medals, four bronze medals, and two honorable mentions—and helped to solidify the importance of material culture in the fight for African American civil rights. Though the Niagara Movement achieved few tangible results, many of its participants, such as Du Bois, Trotter, and Ida B. Wells-Barnett, helped form the National Negro Committee in 1909 in the wake of racial violence that had occurred in Springfield, Illinois, in 1908. The goal of that interracial organization was to end racial discrimination and inequality. At its 1910 meeting, the National Negro Committee became the National Association for the Advancement of Colored People.[17]

On May 15, 1916, Jesse Washington—age seventeen—was lynched in front of a thousand spectators, burned, and left hanging for several days in downtown Waco, Texas. In July of

1.9
"NAACP Anti-Lynching
Committee Stop Lynching"
pinback, .75", 1916–19

that year, the NAACP established an anti-lynching committee
to develop a public awareness campaign and a strategy to end
the barbaric practice through federal legislation [FIGURE 1.9].
Led by NAACP field secretary James Weldon Johnson,
assistant field secretary Walter White, and executive secretary
John Shillady, the committee began a campaign to investigate
the history of lynching in America, to educate the public
about the practice, and to rally the support of white politicians
who would potentially back anti-lynching legislation.[18]
The committee published lynching statistics and took out
advertisements in newspapers, noting that 3,436 people
were lynched between 1889 and 1922.[19] In spring 1919, after
exhaustive research, the committee published the book
Thirty Years of Lynching in the United States, which tallied
more than 2,500 lynchings since 1889.

The NAACP championed a philosophy of achieving
equality through legislation and the courts. The efforts paid
off in April 1918, when two Republican congressmen, Leonidas

Dyer from St. Louis and Merrill Moores from Indianapolis, introduced anti-lynching legislation to Congress. The basis for the bill was that the failure of local officials to protect citizens from lynching denied victims the equal protection under the law due to them under the Fourteenth Amendment. That same year, Shillady also started planning a national conference on lynching. Sadly, the legislation was not passed, but the campaign was successful in recruiting new members to the NAACP. These efforts allowed the organization to grow and served as a template for future campaigns.[20]

The NAACP became the leading civil rights organization in the United States. As membership swelled, the NAACP's campaign to end lynching, segregation, and disenfranchisement intensified. Material culture was central to those efforts. Members wore pins [FIGURE 1.10] to show their support for the NAACP's agenda and to recruit new members into the organization. Many of the early NAACP meetings were held in the Sharp St. Methodist Church in Baltimore, Maryland. The congregation was established in 1787 and was involved in the abolitionist movement. It founded schools for African Americans after the Civil War and was known as the "Mother Church" for Black Methodism. By wearing a badge [FIGURE 1.11], members of Sharp St. Methodist Church could show their affiliation with the history and mission of this congregation.[21]

The NAACP knew that in order to achieve its goals, it had to grow. Objects were produced to publicize a membership drive in 1918, which became known as the "Moorfield Storey Drive" (Moorfield Storey was the first president of the NAACP in 1909 until his death in 1929). The drive aimed to recruit fifty thousand members, which would be a fivefold increase. Shillady met with Storey and organized the membership drive around Storey's seventieth birthday. The effort was publicized in multiple editions of *The Crisis*, the NAACP's quarterly publication, and the language demonstrates the dramatic and immediate need for funds to aid in the fight against lynching:

1.10
NAACP membership pin, .75", 1911
1.11
Sharp St. Methodist Church Member badge, 2.5 x 3.5", early twentieth century

March 1918, vol. 15, no. 15

Many have asked how best can the members of the Association express their appreciation of Mr. Storey's achievement and adequately celebrate this great victory. Some members and several branches wished to tender to Mr. Storey a public dinner or a testimonial meeting; but obviously this cannot be done in ninety places at which Mr. Storey could be present in person. Mr Storey has let it be known that the kind of tribute he would most appreciate would be a determined drive for a membership large enough to make the Association a greater power throughout the nation. The National Association, therefore, transmits to every branch Mr. Storey's appeal for 50,000 members by May 1, 1918. Mr. Storey says: "Do not hold laudatory meetings. I shall feel best repaid if every branch will join enthusiastically in the effort to secure 50,000 members for the N.A.A.C.P. We need a large membership to ensure the permanent success of our great movement against race prejudice." [22]

May 1918, vol. 16, no. 1

The N.A.A.C.P. has no endowments. It is supported entirely by voluntary contributions and membership fees. It appeals to all fair-minded citizens, white and colored, to join in the effort to secure simple justice under the law for colored citizens.

The Moorfield Storey Drive for 50,000 Members Negroes in many states are disfranchised, discriminated against, "Jim Crowed," lynched, denied equal protection of the laws, equaleducational advantages for their children, and equal economic opportunity. National honor demands justice for all citizens. [23]

The Moorfield Storey Drive and the objects produced to support it were a way to recruit new members, raise money, and focus the public's attention on the scourge of lynching

1.12
NAACP Moorfield Storey
Drive pinback, .75",
1917–18

1.13
**E. G. Renesch, WWI framed
poster, 13.75 x 18.75", 1919**

across the United States [**FIGURE 1.12**]. The language of the recruitment was patriotic, invoking the growing awareness of America's potential involvement in World War I. In this campaign, the NAACP learned a valuable lesson about how the material culture it produced could increase membership while promoting the organization's many causes.

Although the anti-lynching Dyer bill was defeated in Congress, recruitment efforts continued within the NAACP through World War I, and its numbers steadily grew. The organization did not just reach its goal of increasing membership to fifty thousand—it exceeded it. Its publicity campaign and the sale of pinbacks caused membership to

surge. In 1912, there were 329 members. In 1916, there were 8,785, and by 1919, there were 91,203 members of the NAACP.[24]

The United States entered World War I on the side of the Allied powers in 1917, and the reaction from African American leaders varied from patriotic support for the war effort to condemnation of the war as serving only to advance capitalist interests. W. E. B. Du Bois and the NAACP rallied behind President Woodrow Wilson's message that the goal of the war was to "make the world safe for democracy." The NAACP argued that its objectives remained the same during the war but its efforts should be focused on achieving victory. That strategy for victory was to campaign for Black soldiers to participate fully in the war effort.[25]

But there were shocking disparities between America's message and its actions, which were emphasized by Chandler Owen and A. Philip Randolph (the editors of the monthly magazine *The Messenger*) and other Black leaders on the left. In a letter to President Wilson, they stated, "Lynching, Jim Crow, segregation, discrimination in the armed forces and out, disenfranchisement of millions of Black souls in the South— all these things make your cry of making the world safe for democracy a sham, a mockery, a rape of decency and travesty of common justice." The NAACP argued that the Unites States should make good on its promise to advance democracy by achieving it, most importantly, at home.[26]

More than 380,000 Black soldiers served in the armed forces during World War I, and more than 2.3 million registered for the draft, but because of strict segregation laws, most were relegated to support and service rolls. Most Black servicemen dug trenches, handled supplies, serviced officers, and buried the dead. Only forty-two thousand African American soldiers saw combat; many more certainly would have served if given the opportunity. Black regiments remained segregated, but under pressure from the NAACP, two Black combat divisions were created and Black officers were trained at a segregated camp in Des Moines, Iowa.[27]

1.14 (ABOVE)
"Don't Tread on Me" 369th Regiment pin, .5 x .5", 1918
1.15 (OPPOSITE)
"Lieut. James Reese Europe and His Famous 369th U.S. Infantry 'Hell Fighters' Band" songbook, 9.5 x 12", 1915

1.16
"Good Bye Alexander, Good
Bye Honey Boy" songbook,
10.5 x 13.5", 1919

Black regiments and Black officers faced discrimination and ridicule and were allowed to command only Black troops. They were often given inadequate provisions and even traveled in the hull of transport ships as they made their way to the battlefields of Europe. Those Black soldiers who were given the opportunity to fight were often given the toughest and most undesirable assignments, and yet, despite this discrimination, they proved themselves more than able to perform their duties. The poster "True Blue" [FIGURE 1.13] was produced to honor the sacrifice of African American soldiers who fought, and often died, in the war effort. The image shows a mother and three children gazing at a portrait of her husband in uniform, alongside portraits of President Wilson and the Great Emancipator, Abraham Lincoln. The message of the image was that African Americans were patriotic Americans who were sacrificing for the war and should have their constitutional rights protected.[28]

In March 1918, Harlem's Fifteenth Regiment of the New York Army National Guard was redesignated the 369th Regiment, to serve in France. Upon arrival, they were relegated to labor service, but that soon changed. In April, the Army decided to require the 369th to serve in the French Army rather than letting an all-Black combat regiment serve alongside whites in the trenches. The 369th, known as the Harlem Hell Fighters, were not only noteworthy in the trenches but also became symbols of the fight for democracy across the globe and on the home front. They served alongside the French Army a record 191 days on the front. Their bravery and prowess in battle became widely acknowledged on both sides of the trenches—so much so that the entire unit was awarded the Croix de Guerre, the French command's highest military honor, along with two other all-Black regiments. The pin in FIGURE 1.14 is the 369th Regiment's insignia and was worn by the Harlem Hell Fighters in France, as well as once they returned home. It was a symbol of their sacrifice, patriotism, and desire to be treated as equal citizens in the country whose ideals they helped defend.[29]

No African American soldiers received medals during World War I from the United States, but the French people embraced African American soldiers and the culture they brought with them. Among them was the 369th Regimental Band, led by New Yorker James Reese Europe, who introduced many Black composers to the French [FIGURE 1.15]. The band continued to perform upon its return to the United States but was not allowed to march in the victory parade in New York City. The Harlem Hell Fighters Band toured around the United States, the members' patriotism a demonstration of the sacrifice African Americans made for the Allies during the war as well as a reminder that they did not have access to the democracy they had helped to defend.[30]

Despite the efforts of men like the Harlem Hell Fighters, discrimination against Black soldiers continued after the war. There was no movement toward civil rights by elected

(FROM TOP TO BOTTOM)
1.17
NAACP membership pinback, .75", 1921
1.18
NAACP Life Member tack, .5", 1920s
1.19
NAACP pinback, .5", 1920s
1.20
NAACP Lieut. pinback, .75", 1920s

officials, and as segregation, lynching, and disenfranchisement continued unabated, organizations such as the NAACP linked the fight for democracy abroad to the fight against Jim Crow at home. The songbook in **FIGURE 1.16** drew on patriotic sentiment to bring attention to the enlistment of African American soldiers. It sent a message to white Americans: the striking graphics depicted African American soldiers as heroes deserving civil rights as contributors to the defense of the freedom that they themselves did not enjoy.

In the spring and summer of 1919, a wave of attacks on African Americans were committed by whites across the country. Despite the efforts of hundreds of thousands of Black servicemen, and millions on the home front, there was a violent backlash to the assertion that democracy should include African Americans. White mobs attacked African Americans in dozens of cities—large and small, urban and rural—including Washington, DC; Chicago; St. Louis; Charleston, South Carolina; and Elaine, Arkansas, where more than two hundred were killed. The NAACP focused on the violence in *The Crisis*, where Du Bois wrote a stirring text about fighting for democracy in a country that does not believe you should participate in it:[31]

> **This country of ours, despite all its better souls have done and dreamed, is yet a shameful land.**
>
> It *lynches*....
> It *disfranchises* its own citizens....
> It encourages *ignorance*....
> It *steals* from us....
> It *insults* us....
> We *return*.
> We *return from fighting*.
> We *return fighting*.

Make way for Democracy! We saved it in France, and by the Great Jehovah, we will save it in the United States of America, or know the reason why.[32]

During its first ten years, the NAACP learned how producing pinbacks, tacks, buttons, and badges could work toward achieving its objectives, as well as to increase membership and revenue. A 1921 NAACP pinback [FIGURE 1.17] represented one's belief in equality, which became a badge of honor and a source of recruitment, although it also, in many instances, was used as a pretext for white hostility.

The NAACP's membership peaked in the aftermath of World War I to one hundred thousand by 1923 in 450 branches nationwide. An internal review noted that local branches contributed less than half of the annual NAACP budget of $55,000 and that some branches were inactive. Membership began to wane after that, and James Weldon Johnson, who in 1920 became the first African American executive secretary of the NAACP, and the NAACP's national director, Robert Bagnall, began a new concerted effort to raise money and membership. Fieldworkers solicited contributions, and members were asked to contribute $5 to $10 for an annual membership. Life memberships were created for $1,000, and funds, as well as membership, rapidly increased [FIGURES 1.18–1.20].[33]

Many different visions for Black liberation developed alongside the integrationist strategy of the NAACP. As the NAACP focused on achieving Black equality in the United States through the court system and legislative action, many Black organizations, such as Marcus Garvey's Universal Negro Improvement Association (UNIA), promoted the unity of all African peoples worldwide, known as Pan-Africanism, and called for African Americans to either return to Africa or to create independent Black communities separate from whites.[34]

The UNIA was founded in Kingston, Jamaica, in 1914. It relocated its headquarters to Harlem, New York City, in

1.21
Hon. Marcus Garvey
Provisional President
of Africa pinback, 1.25",
1920–21

1916, at which time it claimed two million members in thirty
chapters in the United States and the West Indies. In August
1921, the UNIA held its first International Convention of
the Negro Peoples of the World in Madison Square Garden,
followed by a parade through Harlem. By the end of that year,
it claimed four million members worldwide.[35]

During the convention, the UNIA adopted a national flag
with the colors red, black, and green and elected officials for
its provisional government. Marcus Garvey was elected as the
provisional president of the African Republic, while James
W. H. Eason was named Leader of the American Negroes.
Responding to the discrimination during WWI and persistent
racism during the 1920s, Garvey's vision for Black liberation
was more militant than that of groups such as the NAACP.[36]

Followers of Marcus Garvey and his philosophy of Black
nationalism and Pan-Africanism were known as "Garveyites."
They emphasized racial unity and pride, self-reliance, and

separation from whites rather than integration. Their material culture (banners, badges, pinbacks, and military-style uniforms) was the primary way by which the UNIA proclaimed their message to the public, and was effective in garnering supporters. Banners at the 1921 convention read "We want a Black Civilization," and Garvey proclaimed, "I am appealing to those who are loyal and true, to stick solidly by and victory will perch upon the banners of the Universal Negro Improvement Association."[37]

Key to Garvey's ideas for Black nationalism was economic self-determination. The UNIA-sponsored Negro Factories Corporation began many business ventures such as hotels, restaurants, retail stores, and manufacturers. A fleet of ocean liners—the Black Star Line—was envisioned as the cornerstone of this endeavor; it was planned to provide a physical link between Africa and the Americas and also to serve as a spiritual and psychological link among African peoples across the globe.[38]

Stocks in the Black Star Line were sold for $5 a share. By 1922, more than 150,000 had been sold, but the three ships purchased proved to be unseaworthy and the Black Star Line was a complete failure as a business venture. The US Department of Justice began investigating Marcus Garvey and the UNIA, as they were doing with many left-wing organizations. Garvey was convicted of mail fraud for selling bogus stocks through the mail and was sentenced to five years in prison, but he was deported to Jamaica in 1927 as an "undesirable alien."[39]

The UNIA was the most popular movement led by African Americans prior to World War II, and Garvey's ideas persisted into the modern Civil Rights Movement. Regalia was particularly significant to Garveyites, who wanted to portray Garvey as the savior of his race and the UNIA as an influential and powerful organization on par with national governments. Their military-style uniforms conveyed legitimacy in the eyes of their opponents as well as pride to their supporters.

1.22
**NAACP Delegate badge
with ribbon, 2 x 4.5", 1926**

1.23
"Abolish Poll Tax 100% Democracy" pinback, .75", 1930s

By wearing these uniforms in public, along with buttons, ribbons, and pinbacks [FIGURE 1.21], and by flying banners, the UNIA was able to garner public attention, recruit new members, raise revenue, and solidify their identity as the preeminent Black organization of the early twentieth century.

Anti-lynching campaigns continued throughout the 1920s in the face of increasing violence and hostility toward African Americans. The efforts of the NAACP were vindicated when the House passed the Dyer bill, 230 to 119, on January 26, 1922. There was tremendous backlash to the bill, which was filibustered in the Senate and died in committee without being voted on. Congressman Dyer introduced a new anti-lynching bill in the House in December 1925, which was followed by the introduction of another bill in the Senate by William B. McKinley. In February 1926, James Weldon Johnson testified before the subcommittee of the Senate Judiciary Committee on behalf of the McKinley bill and submitted facts on lynching.[40]

In 1926, the NAACP met in Chicago for its seventeenth annual conference and continued to place the passage of anti-lynching legislation at the top of its agenda [FIGURE 1.22]. Although federal anti-lynching legislation had not been passed, the NAACP had learned not only valuable lessons about lobbying and the legislative process but also how to influence public opinion through material culture.[41]

Alongside the NAACP's mission to pass anti-lynching legislation was its campaign against poll taxes. The NAACP had campaigned against these taxes since its founding, but its efforts intensified in the 1930s. After the Civil War and the passage of the Fifteenth Amendment, white supremacists devised multiple ways to disenfranchise Black voters. These included literacy tests, "grandfather clauses," the "white primary" (in which only whites were allowed to vote), and poll taxes. The NAACP first used the courts to challenge the constitutionality of grandfather clauses in 1910, after Oklahoma passed one such constitutional amendment, declaring that only those whose grandfathers could vote in 1865 could vote. The NAACP convinced US Attorney General James Clark McReynolds that this violated the Fifteenth Amendment, and it filed a challenge in 1913 that reached the Supreme Court in 1915. Moorfield Storey, working for the NAACP, was able to persuade the justices, and in *Guinn v. United States,* the Supreme Court declared that grandfather clauses were unconstitutional.[42]

This success convinced the NAACP to mount legal challenges to poll taxes and white primaries, which were the most effective methods to keep African Americans from voting. At the 1925 NAACP convention, the organization decided to focus on those two tactics, in particular the white primaries in Texas. It filed multiple suits and argued cases before the Supreme Court in 1921, 1927 (*Nixon v. Herndon*), 1932 (*Nixon v. Condon*), and 1935 (*Grovey v. Townsend*). The NAACP needed money to mount these legal challenges, and the sale of objects like the pinback in FIGURE 1.23 helped to sustain this legal strategy. Their efforts eventually paid off with *Smith v. Allright* in 1944, when the Supreme Court declared white primaries unconstitutional.[43]

During the Great Depression, many labor unions and leftist organizations included protecting the rights of African Americans in their platforms. They linked the fight for workers' rights and solidarity across the world to African Americans' struggle against Jim Crow at home. The National Domestic Workers Union organized in Harlem to end the practice of "slave markets," where Black women gathered on street corners in the hopes of being picked by white women for a day's domestic service. The American Federation of Labor initially resisted the creation of the Brotherhood of Sleeping Car Porters in 1925, but through the efforts of the Brotherhood's president, A. Philip Randolph, the AFL recognized the union in 1935.

Randolph joined the Socialist Party of America in the 1920s, but racism within the ranks limited membership in that party largely to a circle of intellectuals in Harlem.[44] The Communist Party of the United States of America gained credibility among many African Americans in the 1930s, due to its rejection of Jim Crow and its campaign against what it called a "legal lynching" in Paint Rock, Alabama. While on a train stop in 1931, two white women falsely accused nine Black teenagers of rape. The accused were arrested, jailed, and later moved to nearby Scottsboro, Alabama, due to fears that they would be lynched. The "Scottsboro Boys," as they were dubbed in the press, were nonetheless sentenced to death by an all-white jury. The legal arm of the Communist Party, the International Labor Defense (ILD) took up the case and began a campaign to raise money for the Scottsboro case. The ILD sold stamps for just one cent and allowed many more supporters to contribute. The stamps could be placed in a booklet distributed by the ILD, which contained information about the case, the defendants, and the fight against Jim Crow.[45]

The May 1933 issue of the ILD's magazine, *Labor Defender,* announced the campaign to use the stamps [FIGURE 1.24] to raise money for their defense. "Send to day—to the Scottsboro New Trial Emergency Fund of the International Labor Fund for some of these stamps." The campaign was successful in generating money for the legal expenses and publicizing the pervasiveness of lynching, but it took decades, and two Supreme Court appearances, for all nine defendants to be fully acquitted.[46]

The NAACP's Legal Defense and Educational Fund (LDF) was created in 1940 to serve as the legal branch of the organization, although money and awareness had been raised years prior by objects such as the Stop Lynching pinbacks in FIGURES 1.25 + 1.26, which were given to members who donated to the NAACP in the 1930s. In the process of lobbying for the federal anti-lynching legislation Costigan-Wagner bill, which was defeated, the LDF developed strategies that allowed NAACP attorneys to fight segregation through

1.24 (OPPOSITE)
International Labor Defense "Save the Scottsboro Boys" stamps, .75 x 1" each, 1933

the judicial system, and they gained valuable experience challenging Jim Crow in the courts. The funds raised for the NAACP eventually helped the LDF challenge educational segregation in the 1954 landmark *Brown v. Board of Education* Supreme Court case.[47]

In the February 1938 issue of *The Crisis*, the NAACP announced a "New Crusade for Liberty," featuring a photograph of the pinback in **FIGURE 1.27** with an explanation of its objectives:

1.25 (RIGHT)
NAACP Legal Defense Fund "Stop Lynching" pinback, .75", 1937–39

1.26 (LEFT)
NAACP "Build Democracy Stop Lynching" pinback, .75", 1937–39

1.27 (MIDDLE)
NAACP "New Crusade for Liberty" Diamond Jubilee pinback, 1", 1938

As a fitting observance of the 75th anniversary year of the Emancipation Proclamation, the National Association for the Advancement of Colored People is launching a New Crusade for Liberty whose goal is full citizenship for colored Americans.

The crusade will be launched officially February 1
with the sale of New Crusade buttons throughout the nation
under the direction of Mrs. Daisy E. Lampkin, field secretary
of the N.A.A.C.P. The buttons commemorate the Diamond
Jubilee of Emancipation, 1863–1938, and cite the immediate
objectives as the securing of the ballot for all qualified
citizens and the securing of a just share of public education
for colored children…

The formal announcement of the New Crusade by
the N.A.A.C.P. stated…

"To launch this crusade, to secure funds for
pushing it, and to make known to great numbers of
people the goals which we seek, we are selling a 'New
Crusade' button.

"We appeal to all colored Americans and all friends
of theirs and of liberty and democracy to assist in the
sale of these buttons and to show by the purchase and
wearing of them their belief in the cause." [48]

Material culture began to make an impact on the Civil Rights
Movement in the nineteenth century, and its effects increased
during the early twentieth century. These objects helped civil
rights organizations combat Jim Crow, and the groups' steady
growth in membership and political impact was due, in large
part, to their material culture. The objects reflected the goals
of each organization and were instrumental in achieving them.
Those objectives, such as anti-lynching legislation, were not
always immediately successful, but the objects imparted a
growing sense of a national Civil Rights Movement and were
representative of their times. Civil rights activists understood
the power of these objects and knew they helped get results.
Material culture could inform the public, sway opinions, raise
money, increase membership, and help to form a sense of a
national struggle for change.

NO JIM
CROW
★ IN THE ★

Finish the Fight
(1939–1950)

A s World War II began, most civil rights organizations took the position that the United States should focus on securing democracy at home before it attempted to expand it abroad. African Americans, however, were walking a fine line when they criticized the United States in a time of war. Any critique could be viewed as damaging to the war effort and, in the minds of some civil rights leaders, could delay progress toward civil rights legislation.[1]

Many organizations, such as the AFL, the Congress of Industrial Organizations, and the Knights of Labor, as well as civil rights groups such as the National Urban League and the NAACP, worked toward the passage of legislation to combat lynching, job and housing discrimination, and segregation in the armed forces. Civil rights leaders such as A. Philip Randolph, head of the Brotherhood of Sleeping Car Porters, and Walter White, NAACP executive secretary, believed that eliminating segregation in the military was a way to both aid the war effort and make progress against Jim Crow. Along

with T. Arnold Hill, adviser on Negro affairs for the New Deal agency the National Youth Administration, Randolph and White met with Secretary of the Navy Frank Knox and Under Secretary of War Robert P. Patterson in September 1940 to make the case for eliminating segregation in the armed services.[2]

The meeting did little to persuade President Franklin D. Roosevelt's administration to act, and African Americans had good reason to argue that protecting their civil rights in the United States was a more immediate, and important, goal than defending our allies in Europe. Segregated Army units were permitted to have no Black officers except chaplains and medics, and the Navy announced that African Americans could only serve as stewards, mess attendants, and cooks. The American Red Cross continued the practice of keeping so-called Black blood and white blood separate, which prompted Charles Drew, the African American physician who designed the method for storing and shipping blood plasma, to resign in protest.[3]

Material culture was at the center of these efforts, and it reflected the changing objectives of civil rights organizations as the war progressed. The campaigns, and corresponding objects made for those campaigns, allowed African Americans to show patriotism by calling to uphold American ideals. Buttons, pinbacks, and posters raised awareness, public support, and money that could sustain civil rights organizations in the long fight that lay ahead. The pinback in FIGURE 2.1 was issued by the Communist Party of the United States of America (CPUSA) on May Day (May 1), 1940. May Day had long been a day promoting labor solidarity and was used by civil rights groups to emphasize the relationship among creating jobs at home, staying out of the war, and focusing on legislation to combat lynching and segregation.[4]

President Roosevelt's lack of response to calls for an end to segregation in the military was disappointing, and continued discrimination in the armed forces caused many

2.1
May 1, 1940, "Jobs Peace Civil Rights" pinback, .75", 1940

Black leaders to call for a protest march on Washington. In January 1941, Randolph called for fifty to one hundred thousand Black Americans to gather on July 1 in the nation's capital to demand equality in the defense industries and an end to segregation.[5]

Roosevelt feared how a large rally in the nation's capital would look to the nation's allies, bringing international scrutiny of Jim Crow practices in the United States. Randolph was under tremendous pressure to call off the march, but he knew organized protest was an effective strategy to get the president to act on segregation. Six days before the scheduled march, on June 25, Roosevelt issued Executive Order 8802, which declared, "There shall be no discrimination in the employment industries or government because of race, creed, color, or national origin." The order implemented the Fair Employment Practices Committee (FEPC), which was established to enforce the ban on discrimination in defense industries. In exchange, Randolph called off the march, but during the war, he and other civil rights leaders remained vocal critics of the government's unwillingness to combat racial discrimination on the home front.[6]

A more permanent version of the FEPC was enacted by Congress after the war, due to the temporary committee's lack of action to desegregate the defense industries and to act on instances of discrimination by private defense contractors. The FEPC helped many African Americans get jobs within the defense industry, but the organization did not have the power to punish employers' failure to comply, which was rampant, especially in the South.[7]

The March on Washington Movement produced stamps [FIGURE 2.2] to call for the FEPC to be established by permanent federal legislation, rather than by executive order. Pins and buttons also allowed many to show their support for the enactment of these reforms, but implementation was slow. The pinback in FIGURE 2.3 supports the passage of the Fair Employment Practices Act, which had stalled in Congress

due to conservative opposition. The language and implementation of the FEPA was based on Executive Order 8802, and civil rights activists wore these pinbacks to demonstrate their support for the bill's passage.

Wearing this pinback, and others like it, sent a broader message of defiance to the supporters of Jim Crow, as well as to liberal whites, that an organized, Black-led, mass protest movement was being created. This strategy of linking material culture with the changing focus of the Movement brought public support and legislative successes during, and after, the war.

African American leaders were concerned that their calls for equality at home would be misconstrued as disloyalty, which might set back the fight for civil rights. The Double V campaign, launched in 1942, provided a way to fight racial discrimination while simultaneously contributing to the war effort. On February 7, 1942, the *Pittsburgh Courier* published a letter to the editor from reader James G. Thompson of Wichita, Kansas, that proclaimed, "Let we colored Americans adopt the double VV for a double victory." The first *V* was "for victory over our enemies from without," while the second *V*

2.2 (OPPOSITE)
"Make FEPC Permanent for Jobs & Justice" March on Washington Movement stamps, 1.5 x 2" each, 1948
2.3 (ABOVE)
Fair Employment Practices Act "YES-11" pinback, 1", 1941

stood for "victory over our enemies from within." From that point on, the double V symbol became popular among African Americans as a way to demonstrate their patriotic support for the war as well as their demand for the United States to live up to its own democratic ideal of equality under the law.[8]

The Double V campaign had numerous goals during the war, including the end of segregation in the armed services, the passage of anti-lynching legislation, and the employment of African Americans in wartime industries, and it also provided a foundation of support for the Civil Rights Movement after the war was over. From the entry of the Unites States into the war in December 1941, civil rights leaders planned for the fight that was to come once the Allied Powers won. Roy Wilkins wrote in the March 1942 edition of *The Crisis* that African Americans did not "want to come back to the same old world of the 1930s."[9]

Civil rights organizations understood that winning public support was vital to their efforts both in pressing for equal treatment during the war and in gaining white support afterward—which would be necessary for the passage of civil rights legislation. The material culture of the Double V campaign used imagery that appealed to Americans' patriotism, while also demonstrating that the impetus behind the war—the desire to make the world safe for democracy— was a goal worth fighting for at home.[10]

The shape of the pin in FIGURE 2.4 signified that the United States was becoming a shield for democracy against the forces of fascism across the world. The red, white, and blue color scheme identified the fight for civil rights as a patriotic duty, and the letter V was already familiar to Americans as a sign for victory. The flyer in FIGURE 2.5 used the patriotic symbolism of an African American soldier in uniform and the bald eagle, specifically linking the African American struggle for freedom with the contemporary struggle against fascism, with the rays of sunlight behind the soldier and the eagle's wings forming a subtle double V. And the pinback in FIGURE 2.6 features an

2.4 (ABOVE)
Double V campaign pin, .75 x 1", 1942–44
2.5 (OPPOSITE)
Double V "Let Freedom Ring" flyer, 7 x 9", 1942–45

American eagle behind the double V, with the inscription "Double Victory Abroad—At Home / Democracy." This imagery was very powerful and helped to convince many Americans to support both the enlistment of Black soldiers in the war effort and their equal treatment once they returned home.

Some gains were made by African Americans during the war years, but progress was slow and halting. Black soldiers typically were placed in noncombat roles, and it was not until August 1945 that the US Army integrated its officer training camps, which affected only 1 percent of Black serviceman. Although Roosevelt's Executive Order 8802 established the Fair Employment Practices Committee to investigate complaints of discrimination and address grievances, he crippled the agency from the beginning by providing no mechanism for enforcement, a minuscule budget, and leadership that was unwilling to respond to the grievances of African Americans.[11]

The US Navy did not change its employment policy until 1944. Integration was slow, and Black servicemen and servicewomen continued to face discrimination for the remainder of the war. By the end of the war, 90 percent of the 168,000 Black men employed by the Navy were messmen. The US Marine Corps did not allow Black recruits until 1942 and set up separate training facilities in North Carolina to keep white and Black marines apart. The US Army Air Corps, renamed the US Army Air Forces in 1941 as a distinct military branch, remained segregated throughout the war.[12]

Black women faced similar treatment to men throughout the armed services. More than four thousand Black women volunteered for the Women's Army Corps (WAC), but most were relegated to janitorial duties, while white women did technical and clerical work. The Navy banned Black women altogether from entering its volunteer female unit, Women Accepted for Volunteer Emergency Service (WAVES), until 1944.[13]

2.6 (ABOVE)
"Double Victory Democracy Abroad—At Home" pinback, .75", 1942–45
2.7 (OPPOSITE)
Betsy Graves Reyneau, "Keep us flying!" poster for war bonds depicting Tuskegee Airman Robert W. Deiz, 19.75 x 27.5", 1943

Discrimination against Black soldiers was pervasive in both training and combat. White officers claimed that Black soldiers were not capable of withstanding the rigors of combat, a claim that their service records contradict, as civil rights leaders clearly pointed out. Despite these many indignities, African Americans wanted to serve their country. Civil rights leaders such as Walter White of the NAACP and A. Philip Randolph of the Brotherhood of Sleeping Car Porters lobbied vigorously to allow African Americans to train and serve in every branch of the armed services.

Walter White had a personal friendship with Roosevelt that allowed him to gradually convince the president to permit the training and deployment of Black aviators. In March 1941, the Army Air Corps announced that it would be accepting applicants for an all-Black pursuit squadron, to be trained at the Tuskegee Institute. The NAACP argued that not only should Black soldiers be allowed to fly in combat but also that they had the right to fight for their country in desegregated units, and that the creation and separate training of an all-Black unit was simply a continuation of Jim Crow in the sky. Despite their extensive training, the Ninety-Ninth Pursuit Squadron—Tuskegee Airmen—were denied combat assignments. They eventually saw combat, but many Black aviators, such as the Second Cavalry Division, were relegated to duties such as unloading ships and driving trucks. In 1943, the Treasury Department created a poster featuring Tuskegee Airman Robert William Deiz to encourage the public to buy war bonds [FIGURE 2.7]. The poster, designed by Betsy Graves Reyneau, reminded Americans of the contribution of Black soldiers to the war effort but was also a reminder to many African Americans about the continued racism and segregation they experienced on a daily basis.[14]

African American soldiers continued to grapple with discrimination when they returned home from the war. For example, at Fort Bragg, North Carolina, Black soldiers were forced to ride unreliable buses marked "Colored Troops" and were not allowed to board white-only buses. In towns across the United States returning Black soldiers could not eat at the same restaurants or use the same public facilities that German prisoners of war were allowed to frequent.[15]

World War II created a sense of urgency and opportunity for the advancement of civil rights in the United States. The material culture produced during World War II by civil rights organizations such as the NAACP was so effective that it influenced new groups like the Congress of Racial Equality (CORE), which played a crucial role in direct-action campaigns in the 1950s and '60s.[16] A new interracial civil rights organization, CORE was formed in 1942 in Chicago. Many of its members were associated with the Fellowship of Reconciliation (FOR), a pacifist organization opposed to the United States' entry into the war. The leadership of CORE believed in immediate action on civil rights, and they developed many innovative strategies that would become a template for the postwar Civil Rights Movement, such as sit-ins and voter registration drives.[17]

CORE's founding leaders were James Farmer, its first chairperson; George Houser, a Methodist minister; and Bernice Fisher, the leader of the FOR chapter in Chicago. Bayard Rustin, a member of FOR who became an integral member of CORE, was the driving force behind the adoption of Mahatma Gandhi's use of nonviolent civil disobedience as a way to protest segregation and disenfranchisement in the United States. In 1943, CORE pioneered the tactic of the sit-in when members demanded service at Jack Spratt Coffee House in Chicago, which served only white customers. Their actions inspired many others to do the same, including three students at Howard University in Washington, DC, who in that same year staged a sit-in at a lunch counter near campus that refused to serve Black customers, after James Farmer and Bayard Rustin had visited the city.[18]

CORE's strategies were more confrontational than those employed by groups such as the NAACP, but African

Americans had good reason to demand swifter change. Congress continued to drag its feet on anti-lynching legislation, and CORE made this a key component of their platform in the 1940s. The pinback in FIGURE 2.8 was produced as part of CORE's campaign for the passage of federal anti-lynching legislation. The image of a hangman's noose, accompanied by the phrase "Break the Noose," was a powerful and sobering reminder that despite the United States' claims that the purpose of World War II was to defend democracy, African Americans were dealing with the fascist tactics of white supremacists at home. The organization's acronym, CORE, is also printed on the pinback.

Pinbacks and buttons were not just symbolic baubles but were used to generate revenue for the fledgling organization. From the start of World War II to the end of the conflict, African Americans used material culture to continue their resistance to Jim Crow. Wearing pins, flying banners, and hanging posters helped increase membership in organizations such as CORE and the NAACP and linked the goals for the war effort to the fight for equality at home. It also helped to create a sense of a growing national movement for civil rights.[19]

As the war ended in 1945, civil rights organizations continued to demand democracy for those on the home front. They wanted to link patriotism to civil rights and create the feeling of a shared struggle—the same sense of duty that helped bond the country together to win the war. The pinbacks in FIGURES 2.9 + 2.10 read, "Democracy for All / NAACP." Their red, white, and blue color scheme denotes patriotism, and the scales represent their belief in equality.

World War II was a decisive event in the Civil Rights Movement. The NAACP, whose membership rose from around five thousand in 1940 to around forty-five thousand by the end of the war, issued the pinback in FIGURE 2.11 in 1946 to launch its initiatives with the slogan "Finish the fight."[20] The colors of the pinback are reminiscent of patriotic designs used during the war, and the message was clear that the fight for

2.8
CORE "Break the Noose"
pinback, 1", 1942–43

2.9 (LEFT)
**NAACP "Democracy for All"
pinback, 75", 1945**

2.10 (TOP MIDDLE)
**NAACP "Democracy for All"
pinback, .75", 1945**

2.11 (RIGHT)
**NAACP "Finish the Fight"
pinback, .75", 1946**

2.12 (BOTTOM MIDDLE)
**NAACP "$$$ for Illinois
FEPC-JOBS" pinback,
1.25", 1948**

equality was not over. As a result of the contributions African Americans made to winning the war and the efforts of civil rights organizations, some white Americans began to slowly shift away from supporting Jim Crow, but Black citizens continued to be treated poorly in the armed forces as well as within the rest of American society. Their brave service in the war did not dissuade many white Americans from continuing to use violence to maintain the status quo.

Anger reached a boiling point in 1946, when Army veteran Sgt. Isaac Woodard was beaten and had his eyes gouged out by a white sheriff in South Carolina. After the attack, President Harry S. Truman told NAACP Executive Secretary Walter White, "I had no idea it was as terrible as that. We've got to do something."[21]

The efforts of the 1941 March on Washington Movement began to pay off when Truman formed the President's Committee on Civil Rights in 1946, and the committee's report, *To Secure These Rights*, endorsed a permanent Fair Employment Practices Act, an anti-lynching law, and an end to segregation and discrimination in the military. The pinback in FIGURE 2.12 reinforces the importance of securing gainful employment as the nation demobilized from war. African Americans were hired in modest numbers in the US defense industry—mostly in the Northeast—but civil rights leaders wanted the FEPC to use its powers to combat discrimination in hiring practices, housing, and government contracts. Truman issued Executive Order 9981 abolishing racial discrimination in the United States Armed Forces in 1948, but it took several years for Truman's orders to be fully implemented in the armed forces and decades to be realized to any degree in American society.[22]

After World War II, the NAACP used its growing resources and influence to provide legal counsel in cases involving racial discrimination and housing segregation, as well as to continue to press for the passage of federal anti-lynching legislation. Truman's record on enforcing civil rights is a mixed one, but he succeeded in linking the fight for civil rights to the next great foreign policy struggle of the twentieth century, the Cold War. The president remarked, in reference to expanding democracy and resisting communism around the globe, "If we wish to inspire the peoples of the world whose freedom is in jeopardy...we must correct the remaining imperfections in our practice of democracy." Truman was referring to what the NAACP and other civil rights organizations had been demanding: to finish the fight against the fascist tactics used by the supporters of white supremacy across the United States.[23]

The NAACP and other civil rights organizations continued to work toward an end to segregation and disenfranchisement throughout the 1940s, and support

for their objectives of equality for all Americans gained traction. Pinbacks such as those in FIGURES 2.13–2.16 helped the NAACP raise awareness and funds, which allowed them to continue to apply pressure to enforce Truman's order.

Boxer Joe Louis became a hero to African Americans because of his success in the ring and because his victories repudiated the white supremacist ideology of the Nazi Party, which claimed that the "Aryan race" was superior to Blacks in body and mind. He defeated the Italian boxer Primo Carnera in 1935, which came to have special significance for African Americans after fascist Italy invaded Ethiopia—an African nation that had resisted white colonial rule under the leadership of Emperor Haile Selassie, whom Rastafarians later regarded as the second coming of Christ. He faced a rematch with the German boxer Max Schmeling, who had

2.13 (TOP LEFT)
NAACP Member pinback, 1", 1947
2.14 (TOP RIGHT)
NAACP membership pinback, 1", 1948
2.15 (BOTTOM LEFT)
NAACP 40th Anniversary pinback, 1", 1949
2.16 (BOTTOM RIGHT)
NAACP Member pinback, 1", 1950

61

knocked him out in their first contest in 1936.[24] When Louis defeated Schmeling in front of seventy thousand fans at Yankee Stadium in June 1938, he became a hero to millions more as a symbol of American democracy over fascism.

Louis grew in popularity as he defeated a number of boxers from enemy nations during World War II while serving in the Army as a loyal and patriotic American. Louis's image was used for military recruitment during the war, and after the war his image remained a powerful symbol of patriotism and support for Black equality [FIGURE 2.17].[25]

When African Americans wore a Joe Louis pinback [FIGURE 2.18], they were showing their support not just for a beloved sports hero but for a man who demonstrated both American ideals and the harsh reality of what it meant to live within the confines of Jim Crow.

After the defeat of the Axis powers, the US government began to gear up for the next international struggle: the Cold War that was developing between the United States and the Soviet Union, an ally during World War II. The United States was keen to highlight the American values and institutions that had helped win the war, but only those that would also serve as a model for nations deciding between siding with the United States and Western capitalist democracies or with the Soviet Union and its allies [FIGURE 2.19]. In addition, the public was hungry for patriotic symbols that would make them feel united in victory with other Americans.

A federally sponsored traveling exhibition to be designated the "Freedom Train" was proposed by Attorney General Tom C. Clark as a way to remind Americans of their shared democratic values after the trauma of World War II. President Truman backed the idea, and the Freedom Train carried original versions of the US Constitution, the Declaration of Independence, the Truman Doctrine, and the Emancipation Proclamation across the country. There were no African Americans on the board of directors; A. Philip Randolph was considered, and rejected, for membership.

2.17 (OPPOSITE)
"Pvt. Joe Louis says...
'We're going to do our
part...and we'll win because
we're on God's side'"
poster, 7 x 10.25", 1942
2.18 (TOP)
Joe Louis portrait pinback,
1.75", 1947–50

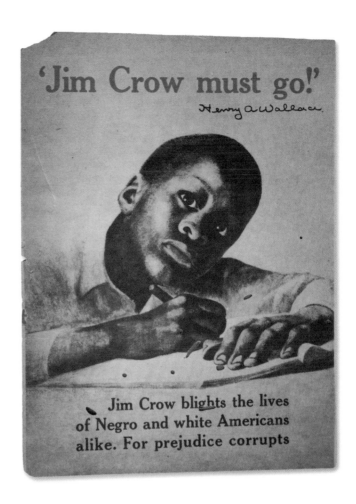

2.19
"Jim Crow must go!" Henry A.
Wallace flyer, 5.5 x 7.25", 1948

The train's first public stop was in Philadelphia, Pennsylvania, on September 17, 1947, and it made more than three hundred stops in the forty-eight contiguous states until its last stop in Washington, DC, on January 22, 1949.[26]

The National Archives provided the historical documents to the nonprofit Advertising Council, which formed the American Heritage Foundation to coordinate the Freedom Train efforts. These included the logistics of travel, as well as the merchandise created to promote it. African Americans were quick to point out the contradictions of the Freedom Train's message as it traveled through states where Blacks and whites were forced to travel in segregated cars. Langston Hughes expressed these sentiments in his 1947 poem, "Freedom Train":

Is there ballot boxes on the Freedom Train?
Do colored folks vote on the Freedom Train?
When it stops in Mississippi will it be made plain
Everybody's got a right to board the Freedom Train.[27]

In September 1947, before the tour's launch, President
Truman announced that people of all races would be allowed
to view the documents on the Freedom Train, but when
cities resisted, the Freedom Train simply skipped those
cities rather than enforce the desegregation order. James J.
Pleasants Jr., mayor of Memphis, Tennessee, sent undercover
agents to other cities in the South where the Freedom Train
was stopping. They reported that viewings were usually
segregated and that when they were not, whites were enraged.
In response, Pleasants stated that there were to be separate
viewing times for African Americans and for whites, and
rather than pressing the issue, the Freedom Train canceled
its stop in Memphis altogether. In Birmingham, Alabama,
public safety commissioner Bull Connor announced that Black
and white attendees would have to wait in different lines and
view the documents separately. The NAACP and other civil
rights organizations threatened to boycott if the Freedom
Train was segregated, and the American Heritage Foundation
canceled the Birmingham stop. The Freedom Train
successfully made it to Montgomery, Alabama, due largely
to the efforts of Rosa Parks, who was then secretary of the
Montgomery NAACP. She published a report criticizing the
all-white train committee and reminded them of the Freedom
Train's national policy of integration. The NAACP's efforts
paid off on December 27, 1947, when the Freedom Train
stopped in Montgomery with an integrated audience.[28]

While the Freedom Train made its way across the United
States, merchandise was created to show support for American
democratic ideals. As civil rights leaders called for the United
States to live up to its own stated founding principles of
freedom, justice, and equality, Freedom Train merchandise

65

was worn and displayed by both white and Black Americans to show their patriotic support for the war effort and also for the values that the founding documents articulated.[29] Souvenirs such as a pennant [FIGURE 2.20], pinback [FIGURE 2.21], pamphlet [FIGURES 2.22 + 2.22A], and ribbon [FIGURE 2.23] were sold to commemorate the tour and to celebrate the end of the war. African Americans wore the pins and hung the pennants as a reminder for Americans to live up to the ideals of democracy professed so profusely after the defeat of the Axis powers. The booklet provided snippets of information about each document brought on the train. African Americans agreed with its message of freedom, justice, and equality under the law but wanted those principles applied to themselves.[30]

The Freedom Train's message retained its association with civil rights into the 1950s and '60s, and in the '70s, the souvenir buttons were reissued for sale to the public. The Mt. Zion Freedom School in Benton County, Mississippi, published a newsletter, the *Benton County Freedom Train*, from October 1964 through December 1965, with a single issue in 1966. This newsletter published information about Freedom Schools, which trained volunteers for voter registration drives but also included poetry from authors such as Langston Hughes. Freedom Schools were established by members of the Student Nonviolent Coordinating Committee during the 1964 Freedom Summer. They were intensive six-week programs that taught children, parents, and grandparents academic subjects including arithmetic, literature, and history, and also provided training on voter

2.20 (TOP)
**Freedom Train pennant,
16 x 5", 1947**
2.21 (LEFT)
**Freedom Train "Our Common
Heritage Freedom Is Our Job"
pinback, 1.5", 1947**
2.22 (OPPOSITE TOP LEFT)
**"The Documents on the
Freedom Train" pamphlet
(front cover), 4.75 x 7.5", 1947**
2.22A (OPPOSITE TOP RIGHT)
**"The Documents on the
Freedom Train" pamphlet
(back cover), 4.75 x 7.5", 1947**
2.23 (OPPOSITE BOTTOM)
**"Ashland Welcomes Freedom
Train Day" ribbon, 2.75 x 8",
1948**

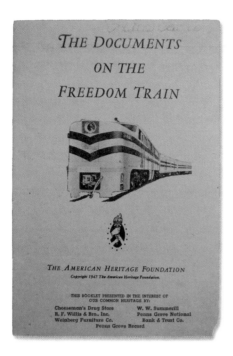

registration, getting voters to the polls, and filling out ballots. More than 2,500 people attended classes in forty Freedom Schools across Mississippi.

The image of the Freedom Train was used to convey a message that African Americans wanted nothing more than the rights guaranteed to them in the Constitution but that those rights were being systematically denied; in 1964, there were no African Americans registered to vote in Benton County.[31]

Understanding the power of material culture to mold public opinion and shape the discourse about civil rights influenced the strategies of civil rights organizations for decades to come. In the 1940s, long-standing civil rights groups, such as the NAACP and the Urban League, as well as new ones, such as CORE, learned how to utilize pins and buttons, flyers and posters, pennants and mailers to achieve many civil rights victories. The fight was far from over, but the strategies developed during these war years helped them on the civil rights battlefields to come.

STAMP
MISSISSIPP

GEOR
LA
EMP
CLIN

JOIN
NA

CHAPTER THREE

Segregation and Desegregation
(1951–1959)

I n the wake of World War II, the fight against segregation intensified, and the NAACP led the charge in 1951, when it combined five legal cases against educational segregation into one class-action suit known generally as *Brown v. Board of Education of Topeka*. The case was aimed at the substandard education offered to African American children, but the broader objective for civil rights leaders was to strike at the entire system of segregation. The NAACP used pinbacks [**FIGURES 3.1–3.4**] and mailers to generate revenue for its Legal Defense and Education Fund, whose attorneys, under the leadership of Thurgood Marshall, began arguing the case before the Supreme Court in 1952.

In December 1952, Marshall and his team opened arguments that segregation was inherently unequal and that it caused harm to Black children. The justices asked the two sides to return in June 1953, but hearings were again postponed until December 1953. Attorneys were instructed to answer

OPPOSITE
NAACP leaders hold a poster that reads "Stamp Out Mississippi-ism! Join NAACP." From left: Henry L. Moon, director of public relations; Roy Wilkins, executive secretary; Herbert Hill, labor secretary; and Thurgood Marshall, special counsel, 1956

(FROM TOP TO BOTTOM)

3.1
**NAACP Member pinback,
.75", 1951**

3.2
**NAACP Member pinback,
.75", 1952**

3.3
**NAACP Member pinback,
.75", 1953**

3.4
**NAACP Member pinback,
.75", 1954**

questions about how the Fourteenth Amendment applied to school segregation. With the help of more than two hundred lawyers, social scientists, and historians, Marshall argued that the intent of the Fourteenth Amendment was to eradicate state-sponsored discrimination. Both sides then had to wait until the court crafted its decision.[1]

In the interim, members and prospective members of the NAACP were sent mailers outlining its strategy for combating segregation. In March 1954, the NAACP's "Guidepost to Freedom" mailer [FIGURES 3.5 + 3.5A] was sent to thousands of homes across the United States. It folded out to a large display detailing the extent of segregation throughout the United State in areas such as housing, transportation, and education. Mailers such as this helped the NAACP raise the funds that led to the success of Marshall's legal team two months later, and the money was also used in subsequent legal challenges in the years ahead. The mailer appealed to readers to join the NAACP with the objective of combating segregation. Its reverse side states, "Join Today - - - Progress Costs Money." It notes that the funds raised by the members reading the mailer were necessary for upholding the democratic ideals the Allies fought to defend in World War II, and that the fight would continue:

> Further progress will cost more money. With the eyes of the world upon America for democratic leadership, the task ahead is gigantic. To those who distrust the United States because of mistreatment of minority groups, we must prove ourselves. Discrimination and segregation must be wiped out. The NAACP needs financial and moral support of every freedom-loving individual and group if this goal is to be achieved.

These mailers directly contributed to the successful outcome in *Brown v. Board of Education* and increased support for the cause of supporting civil rights; they also fostered the sense of a growing national movement.

THE RIGHT TO WORK IS BASIC

Man must work if he is to eat. Denying a man a good job because of his race is denying him the very basis of existence. Largely through the efforts of NAACP branches, fair employment laws have been passed in eleven states – but *thirty-seven states have still refused to do anything about job discrimination*. For this reason, the NAACP believes that FEPC, which means that all citizens would have the opportunity to secure jobs on the basis of merit – not color or religion, is the keystone of the federal civil rights program. All the resources of the Association are pledged to the campaign for establishment of a federal fair employment practices commission with full enforcement powers.

LYNCHING IS NOT DEAD

Contrary to some popular opinion, the fight against lynching is by no means at an end. In recent years, murder by rope and faggot – drastically reduced by the spotlight of shame flashed upon it by the NAACP – has given way to other forms of violence. Bombings, floggings, and shootings have gone unpunished in many sections of the country. The NAACP seeks not only a strong federal anti-lynching law, but also safeguards against police brutality, unconstitutional arrests, and other deprivations of civil liberties.

A FREE BALLOT
. . . Democracy's Lifeblood

Recognizing that Negro Americans, voting in free elections, can contribute to winning the rights and privileges guaranteed to them under our Constitution, the NAACP has geared its legal, legislative, and educational programs toward a vast expansion of the Negro vote. There is still a mammoth job ahead. The legal staff, which cleared the way for Negro voting in the South with Supreme Court victories outlawing "white primaries" and other subterfuges, is taking court action wherever Negroes are still disfranchised.

On the legislative front, the Association is pressing for a federal anti-poll tax law, elimination of unfair registration requirements, and protection for Negro citizens against intimidation in polling places. The NAACP has also undertaken an ambitious educational campaign designed to increase awareness among Negro citizens of the value of their vote, and to encourage the exercise of this basic American right and duty.

OUR CHILDREN'S EDUCATION

Experts have shown that many Negro children are unable to take proper advantage of new opportunities available to them with the cracking of racial barriers in graduate and professional schools, simply because their inadequate grade school training does not qualify them for acceptance by institutions of higher learning. Other experts have shown that segregated schools do not offer Negro children education equal in any respect to that provided white children. The NAACP has launched a full-scale legal attack aimed at abolition of the separate public school system. Just as in the legal battle against segregation in state-supported graduate and professional schools, years of work and countless dollars must go into the struggle at the elementary and high school levels.

THE MEN IN UNIFORM

Who deserves more to enjoy the fruits of democracy than the man who risks his life for it? By exposing injustices against Negro servicemen and working for their correction, the NAACP has brought about a sharp decrease in the amount of discrimination in the armed forces. Publication of the results of an investigation of bias against Negro troops in Japan and Korea by the Association's special counsel led directly to the liquidation of the all-Negro 24th Division and abolition of segregation in the Army in Korea. The Air Force and Navy have led in the elimination of segregation and the Army has taken steps forward, with racial integration extending in some measure to the European front.

HOUSING IS THE ROOT of the EVIL

The ghetto pattern in housing is a vital factor in maintaining segregated education in many Northern areas, and is directly responsible for overcrowding that contributes to crime and disease, and for many other disadvantages that befall minority groups. Despite legal victories invalidating restrictive covenants and city residential segregation ordinances, private builders (even though federal funds make their projects possible) still discriminate against Negroes. A very small percentage of new housing is available to Negro families. The menace of the hate-bomb, with its wake of death and destruction, exists almost everywhere that bigots find no legal means of protecting the "lily-white" character of residential areas. One of the major tasks ahead of the NAACP is the breaking down of Jim Crow housing and the firm establishment of the right of every citizen to live in the home of his choice.

THE TRAVEL NUISANCE

Although the Association has made history in the courts with legal cases which in effect outlawed segregation in interstate travel, a crazy-quilt pattern of Jim Crow in public transportation still plagues travelers. Segregated waiting rooms, sanitary facilities and eating places at airports and terminals cause discomfort, inconvenience, and humiliation to Negro passengers. They also cause embarrassment to our country when foreign visitors who happen not to be white are affected. The NAACP is working for enactment of federal legislation correcting these nuisance Jim Crow practices and is fighting them in the courts.

RECREATION and PUBLIC ACCOMMODATION

Jim Crow in recreational facilities and places of public accommodation has thus far not been challenged consistently enough. Hotels, restaurants, theaters, parks, playgrounds, beaches, swimming pools, and golf courses draw the color line almost wherever and whenever they choose. A new precedent was set at the NAACP's 43rd Annual Convention in Oklahoma City, with the announcement of a full scale attack against segregation in intra-state transportation and recreational facilities.

EQUAL TREATMENT in the COURTS

Much progress has been made in securing the right of every citizen to a fair trial and equal treatment by the courts, but regrettably recent events have shown that a sheriff can still shoot Negro prisoners and escape with impunity by claiming "self-defense," a Negro can be tried for "assault" for looking at a white girl 75 feet away, and a Negro can be put to death for a crime for which no white man ever pays a similar penalty.

AN INTERNATIONAL LEADER

The NAACP is an international leader for human rights, opposing racial injustice wherever it appears. It supports the United Nations, opposes colonialism and imperialism in every form, and musters support for oppressed peoples, whether they be in India, South Africa, Tunisia, Indonesia, or anywhere else. Its activities are closely followed all over the world, particularly in countries where the populations are largely non-white. News of the Association's conferences, legal cases, and other activities is widely disseminated by the Voice of America.

3.5 (TOP)

NAACP "Guidepost to Freedom" pamphlet (front cover), 8.75 x 4", 1954

3.5A (BOTTOM)

NAACP "Guidepost to Freedom" pamphlet (interior), 8.75 x 4", 1954

The Supreme Court justices were swayed by NAACP attorneys Thurgood Marshall, George E. C. Hayes, and James Nabrit Jr.'s argument that segregation violated the equal protection clause of the Fourteenth Amendment and that the 1896 *Plessy v. Ferguson* decision, which established the "separate but equal" doctrine, was unconstitutional. On May 17, 1954, the court handed down a unanimous decision, ruling that segregation solely on the basis of race violated African American children's Fourteenth Amendment rights. The ribbon in **FIGURE 3.6** was produced by an unidentified maker to commemorate this landmark decision and was likely worn in the following years to commemorate this event.[2]

Many Black leaders hailed the decision as the greatest civil rights victory of the century, but jubilation over the *Brown* decision was quickly tempered by the backlash to it. Desegregation was slow or nonexistent, and school districts around the country found ways around the court's decision. In 1955, the Supreme Court heard the case again and ruled that integration should occur with "all deliberate speed." The language pleased the supporters of the decision but was used to delay and prevent the process of desegregation. The button in **FIGURE 3.7** features the phrase "I'm Frontlash" and was worn by supporters of the *Brown* decision in opposition to the "backlash" to school integration.[3]

3.6 (TOP)
17th of May 1954 ribbon,
5 x 1", date unknown
3.7 (BOTTOM)
"I'm Frontlash" button,
1", 1950s

In Prince Edward County, Virginia, authorities said the ruling meant they did not have to integrate, and when a court ruling ordered them to do so in 1959, the county closed its schools until 1964. White students were allowed to attend segregated "academies," while Black students were left without an education. Eventually, in *Griffin v. County School Board of Prince Edward County*, the Supreme Court ruled that its public vouchers for the all-white private schools violated the equal protection clause of the Fourteenth Amendment.[4]

Throughout these uncertain times, civil rights activists continued to use buttons, pinbacks, mailers, flyers, and posters to raise money for organizations, to increase awareness about issues facing African Americans, and to publicly express their support for the cause and their opposition to racist policies. The NAACP was at the forefront of this strategy and produced even more items after *Brown*. Members received annual pinbacks, and in 1959, the NAACP produced a wood and metal stamp to commemorate the organization's fiftieth anniversary [FIGURES 3.8–3.13].

3.8 (TOP LEFT)
NAACP Member pinback, .75", 1955
3.9 (TOP RIGHT)
NAACP Member pinback, .75", 1956
3.10 (BOTTOM LEFT)
NAACP Member pinback, .75", 1957
3.11 (BOTTOM RIGHT)
NAACP Member pinback, .75", 1958
3.12 (ABOVE TOP)
NAACP 50 1909–1959 pinback, .75", 1959
3.13 (ABOVE BOTTOM)
NAACP 50 1909–1959 wood and metal stamp, .75 x .75 x .75", 1959

The enthusiasm created by the *Brown* decision was short-lived, as resistance to desegregation was immediate, sustained, and violent. In 1954 and '55, there was a wave of violence directed at African Americans across the South, including the murder of Emmett Till. The gruesome images of Till's battered corpse, and the acquittal of his two murderers, sparked protests across the United States and, for many, made the struggle for civil rights a national movement.[5]

Emmett Till was fourteen when he was lynched on August 28, 1955, in Money, Mississippi. He was from Chicago and was in the Delta, visiting relatives. For sixty years, Carolyn Bryant maintained that Till whistled at and flirted with her. He did not, but the accusation was a common justification for his murder. Bryant's husband, Roy, and his half-brother, J. W. Milam, abducted Till from his great-uncle's house, beat and tortured the boy, murdered him, and dumped his body in the Tallahatchie River. After his corpse was found three days later, it was sent back to Chicago, where his mother insisted on having an open casket as a testimony to the brutality of Jim Crow.

Sadly, Till's murder was one of thousands of lynchings across the South, but Emmett Till's story galvanized the public in a way not seen before. His young age and innocence, the familiar accusations, the savagery of his injuries, and the press coverage his murder received made Till a symbol of the frustration and perseverance of the fight for freedom and equality for decades to come. When asked what gave her the determination to refuse to give up her bus seat to a white man in Montgomery, Rosa Parks stated, "I thought about

Emmett Till, and I just couldn't." In 1991, Chicago dedicated a seven-mile stretch of Seventy-First Street as Emmett Till Road [FIGURE 3.14] to honor Till and his legacy. The button in FIGURE 3.15 was produced by the Emmett Till Foundation for the dedication and is still worn proudly today.[6]

Despite later setbacks, the *Brown* decision dealt a blow to segregation, and the NAACP went on to lead subsequent efforts to end de facto segregation in the nation's schools, public transportation, accommodations, government, and employment. Other organizations and individuals capitalized on this victory. African American women, in particular, took the lead in the fight to end segregation by organizing meetings, forums, and the grassroots efforts necessary for protests, boycotts, and litigation.[7]

Members of the NAACP gathered in the Sixteenth Street Baptist Church in Birmingham, Alabama, for the first annual Women's Day, on Sunday, September 26, 1954, to discuss the best strategy to end segregation across the South. On the

3.14 (OPPOSITE)
**Emmett Till Rd. sign,
37.5 x 6.75", 1991**
3.15 (ABOVE)
**Emmett Till Day button,
3", 1991**

reverse side of the program belonging to Mae R. Goodrich [FIGURES 3.16 + 3.16A], who gave a solo singing performance about halfway through the meeting, is a handwritten note that reads, "Do you think I should sing 'The House by the Side of the Road'—since seemingly it all points to the words of her speech." Here's an excerpt from the 1928 poem—attributed to Sam Walter Foss—which she may have sung that day:

> Let me live in a house by the side of the road
> Where the race of men go by—
> The men who are good and the men who are bad,
> As good and as bad as I.
> I would not sit in the scorner's seat
> Nor hurl the cynic's ban—
> Let me live in a house by the side of the road
> And be a friend to man.

This meeting, and others like it, helped the NAACP to continue to challenge segregation through the courts. In one case taken up by the organization, Autherine Lucy, a graduate of Miles College in Fairfield, Alabama, wanted to attend graduate school at the University of Alabama, but she knew her application would likely be denied. On June 29, 1955, the NAACP's Thurgood Marshall, Constance Baker Motley, and Arthur Shores secured a court order preventing the University of Alabama from rejecting her application based on her race. Just days later, the court amended the decision to apply to all African American applicants. The Supreme Court upheld the decision on October 10, 1955, but despite these protections, Lucy did not ultimately attend the University of Alabama. On her third day of classes, a violent white mob prevented her from attending, and later that day, the university suspended Lucy on the grounds that they could not provide her a safe environment. She and her legal team filed suit but lost. The University of Alabama expelled Lucy on the basis that the lawsuit slandered the university. Her expulsion was

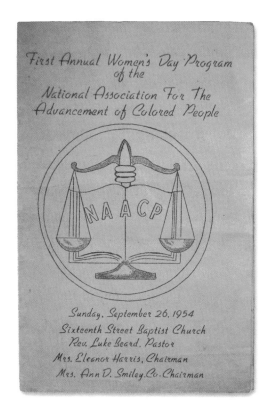

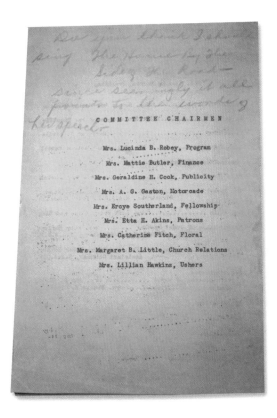

3.16 (LEFT)
NAACP "First Annual Women's Day" program (front cover), 5.5 x 8.5", 1954

3.16A (RIGHT)
NAACP "First Annual Women's Day" program (back cover), 5.5 x 8.5", 1954

overturned by the university in 1980, and she received her master's degree in elementary education in 1992.[8]

Although resistance to the *Brown* decision was widespread, efforts to counter that resistance were even stronger. Across the country, organizations recruited new members, led other direct actions against segregation, and put pressure on local governments. A key tool in these endeavors was their material culture. Pamphlets, pinbacks, buttons, posters, and flyers allowed organizations to spread the word about a growing national Civil Rights Movement with a proven, successful strategy. The poster in **FIGURE 3.17** invited supporters to attend a meeting in Norfolk, Virginia, on February 27, 1958, to honor NAACP Executive Secretary Roy Wilkins. In his speech, Wilkins urged opponents of school integration to end their "massive resistance" campaign,

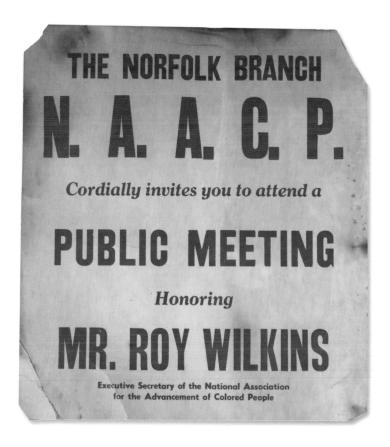

THE NORFOLK BRANCH

N. A. A. C. P.

Cordially invites you to attend a

PUBLIC MEETING

Honoring

MR. ROY WILKINS

Executive Secretary of the National Association
for the Advancement of Colored People

3.17
**NAACP Norfolk Branch
"Public Meeting Honoring
Mr. Roy Wilkins" poster,
13.75 x 15", 1958**

which helped draft legislation to close public schools across
Virginia rather than integrate, taking effect in September
1958. On January 19, 1959, the Virginia Supreme Court struck
down the massive resistance legislation, and on February 2,
1959, the first African American students were admitted to
formerly all-white schools in Arlington and Norfolk.

While the NAACP helped fight for desegregation in
Birmingham, the Women's Political Council, led by Jo Ann
Robinson, planned to boycott the buses of Montgomery,
Alabama. On May 21, 1954, she sent a letter to Mayor W. A.
Gayle demanding that the buses be integrated and declaring
that twenty-four organizations were planning a boycott if the
city did not comply. African American women, who disproportionately relied on public transportation, were particularly
impacted by the discrimination on the city's buses. NAACP

chapters around the country rallied in support of those in
Alabama, confronting segregation through direct action.[9]

NAACP Youth Councils had been initiated by NAACP
Executive Secretary Walter White in 1935. One of their many
objectives was to fight for equal opportunities in education.
These councils were instrumental in Autherine Lucy's efforts
to integrate the University of Alabama, as well as Claudette
Colvin's activism in Montgomery. Colvin, a student at
Booker T. Washington High School and member of her local
NAACP Youth Council, challenged Montgomery's segregated
bus system by refusing to give up her seat to a white passenger
in March 1955. She was arrested, charged, and convicted of
disturbing the peace, violating a segregation law, and assault.
Civil rights attorney Fred Gray filed an appeal on May 6,
1955, to the Montgomery Circuit Court, and the charges of
disturbing the peace and violating the segregation laws
were dropped. Colvin's actions were often overshadowed
by those of her fellow Youth Councilor Rosa Parks, who also
challenged Montgomery's segregated buses months later.[10]

The Rosa Parks of popular memory is an imaginary figure;
Parks's actual role in the Montgomery bus boycott bore little
resemblance to her character as portrayed in publications such
as the comic book *Martin Luther King and the Montgomery
Story*, published by the interfaith civil rights organization the
Fellowship of Reconciliation in 1957 [FIGURE 3.18]. The story of
Rosa Parks as a lone woman who refused to give up her seat to
a white man, sparking a spontaneous boycott, is not an accurate
portrayal of Parks or the boycotts, but it is the story that has
endured. In reality, at the time she was arrested, Parks was a
veteran civil rights activist and organizing for the boycott was
already years in the making.[11]

Rosa Parks was born in Tuskegee, Alabama, in 1913 and
raised in Abbeville by her grandparents, who were active in
the Garvey movement. They instilled in Parks a sense of race
pride and personal dignity. In the 1930s, she married Raymond
Parks, and together, they were active in the campaign to free

the Scottsboro defendants, who had been falsely convicted of rape and sentenced to death in 1931. In 1943, Parks became the secretary of the Alabama chapter of the Brotherhood of Sleeping Car Porters and the Alabama and Montgomery NAACP. During World War II, Parks became an investigator in a series of sexual assault cases in which white men raped Black women. In 1944, she mobilized the Committee for Equal Justice to support assault victim Recy Taylor, and in 1946 helped lead an effort to defend Viola White. White was arrested and beaten by police in Montgomery for refusing to give up her seat on a city bus. She was fined $10, but the courts held off her case indefinitely to avoid a legal challenge to the city's segregation ordinances. In retaliation, A. A. Enger, a white police officer, kidnapped and raped White's sixteen-year-old daughter, who bravely reported the crime to police. NAACP chapter president E. D. Nixon convinced a judge to issue an arrest warrant, but the chief of police tipped off Enger, who fled town and was never charged.

In 1946, Parks went to Highlander Folk School in Tennessee for a workshop that was important to her political development: "Give Light and the People Will Find a Way," led by veteran civil rights activist and SCLC official Ella Baker. In 1949, her friends and allies in Montgomery formed the Citizens Committee for Gertrude Perkins; its members were active in the boycotts a decade later. Gertrude Perkins was twenty-five when she was kidnapped and raped by two white Montgomery police officers while returning home from a bus stop. She went to police to identify her attackers, but the police department refused to hold a lineup or identify which officers were on duty that day. Despite citywide protests, no one was ever charged with the crime.[12]

When Parks refused to give up her seat to a white passenger on December 1, 1955, she was the secretary of the Montgomery branch of the NAACP and had the full backing of civil rights organizations and activists in Alabama, including E. D. Nixon. Following Parks's arrest, Montgomery activists

3.18
Fellowship of Reconciliation, *Martin Luther King and the Montgomery Story* **comic book, 7 x 10.5", 1957**

quickly sprang into action and used material culture to plan the boycott, spread the word, and determine its objectives. On December 2, 1955, Jo Ann Robinson created, mimeographed, and distributed thirty-five thousand flyers calling for a one-day boycott of the city's buses on December 5, 1955. The flyer mentioned the arrest of "Claudette Colbert [*sic*]," noting that it was the "second time…that a negro woman has been arrested for the same thing. This has to be stopped." The Women's Political Council and the NAACP arranged a committee to begin carpools that followed the regular bus routes and picked up residents who were walking. It was very successful, and the city's buses were driven around empty that day.[13]

The need for continuing the boycott was clear, and that afternoon, Black civic and religious leaders in Montgomery, including Ralph Abernathy, Jo Ann Robinson, E. D. Nixon, and Rufus Lewis, met to form the Montgomery Improvement Association (MIA). The meeting was attended by thousands of concerned citizens, and they elected Rev. Dr. Martin Luther King Jr. as their president. It was determined that the boycott would continue until the city's buses were integrated.[14]

The MIA helped organize 325 private cars, 43 dispatch stations, and 42 pickup stations. This preparation and organization allowed the city's residents to continue to travel around Montgomery while exerting economic pressure on the local government to integrate. Meanwhile, the NAACP continued its legal strategy of challenging the constitutionality of Montgomery's bus segregation laws. The NAACP and the MIA determined that Claudette Colvin was a more strategic plaintiff than Rosa Parks, because they feared Alabama officials would hold up Parks's case in the state courts for years. The NAACP Legal Defense and Education Fund approached Colvin, as well as Aurelia Browder, Susie McDonald, Mary Louise Smith, and Jeanetta Reese, to file a case on the basis that they had all been discriminated against by bus drivers enforcing Montgomery's segregation laws.[15]

Although Reese dropped out of the lawsuit amid intimidation by whites, Fred Gray filed the case *Browder v. Gayle* in US District Court on February 1, 1956. In Boston, the Youth Council distributed a newsletter in April 1956 in order to increase awareness about the resistance to integration and the NAACP's struggles against segregation in Montgomery, Philadelphia, Trenton, Boston, and the University of South Carolina [FIGURE 3.19]. This newsletter was used as a recruiting tool and a way to raise money for the NAACP's desegregation efforts across the country. It was given away for free, but it included information on the NAACP's membership drive and

3.19
**Boston Youth Council
newsletter, 8.5 x 14", 1955**

BOSTON YOUTH COUNCIL
FIGHT for FREEDOM   NAACP

Around our Country:

Nationwide Day of Prayer observed March 28, supporting the heroic boycott of the Negroe's of Montgomery, Alabama.

* * *

Roy Wilkins tells 2600 at D.C. Civil Rights meeting that Congress can legislate human rights.

* * *

400 ministers of all religions and races have voiced their support of the Montgomery leaders.

* * *

Representative Adam C. Powell criticized both parties for their weak positions on the question of civil rights. He stated that he and other Negroes are considering joining a 3rd party movement that "would guarantee the equality of the races".

* * *

Students of the Univ. of South Carolina witnessed a blow at freedom of speech when a senior was fired from his job in the State Legislature because of an anti-segregation letter he wrote to the college paper.

* * *

19 Senators and 77 Rep. from 11 deep South states issued a "manifesto" declaring their plans to defy the Supreme Court decision.

* * *

Sen. Henning's Subcommittee approved 4 bills to strengthen Federal protection of civil rights in the spheres of voting new civil rights protection in the Att'y Generals office, to servicemen and a new anti-lynch bill

* * *

Philadelphia City Council passed a unanimous resolution commending Autherine Lucy for her courageous fight.

* * *

Trenton City Commission unanimously adopted a resolution condemning segregation and the arrest of the boycott leaders.

MONTGOMERY U.S.A.

On December 1, 1955 a middle aged Negro woman sitting in the eleventh row on a Montgomery Ala. City Bus was approached by the driver and asked to move to the back because she was violating a city segregation law by sitting so close to the front.

The woman refused and was subsequently arrested and fined $10. Little did the bus driver, the arresting officer, city officials, or even 42 year old Mrs. Rosa Parks know that her steadfast refusal to move to a rear seat would set a spark and ignite beyond hope of extinction decades of smoldering resentment Negroes have harbored against discriminatory, insulting and even viscious treatment on the Mont. City buses.

Within 48 hours after Mrs. Parks arrest and fine, mimeographed hand bills were secretly distributed in Negro areas advising one and all to meet in the areas prominent church to plan a one day boycott of the bus line. the strike was so successful that Negro leaders decided to continue until their demands were met.

Cont'd on page 4

YOUTH HEAR HOWARD

On March 15 and 16, Dr T.R.M. Howard, the staunch civil rights leader from Mt. Bayou Miss., spoke at the Museum of Science, under the auspices of the Boston, NAACP Youth Council and at Harvard under the sponsorhip of the Harvard Society for Minority Rights.

At the museum Youth Council program he asserted that "A time bomb is ticking in Mississippi, and unless
Continued pg 2

Boston Activity Mounts!

EVENTS TO COME:

NAACP mass meeting with Dr. T.R.M. Howard, Negro leader of Miss., April 5 Union Methodist Church.

April 24th, pre-primary election, the NAACP urges you to VOTE!

Youth Council meeting on Sunday, April 8, at 1:30 Freedom House, 14 Crawford St. , Roxbury. We will be holding elections and organizing our Spring projects. Come and join with us.

Youth Council Membership drive begins this month. Our goal, 500 new members

LAST MONTH:

Historic Old North Church site of Boston "Day of Prayer" for the cause of the Alabama boycotters. Sponsored by the Boston Council of Churches, the Rabbinical Assoc. of greater Boston and the interdenominational Ministerial Alliance of Boston. plans were made to every church and synagogue open for prayer.
Cont'd pg. 4

Cooper Comments

To you guys and gals in the Youth Council and to your many readers who missed the Prayer-mass meeting Friday, March 23, and to those of you who were there, Youth really spoke.

Never before have I seen a 25 year old individual who knew his subject, knew how to put it over and hold his audience spellbound to the extent that Attorney Fred D. Grey, Chief Council for the Montgomery Improvement Assoc. did.

Young people and elder people alike are united in
Continued pg 3

NAACP MEMBERSHIP DRIVE – JOIN TODAY

AN IMPORTANT PUBLIC DISCUSSION

"DESEGREGATION and the N.A.A.C.P."

What are the conditions in the South today?

What are the objectives of the N.A.A.C.P.?

What should "Northerners" do — or not do?

Hear These and Other Vital Questions Discussed by:

DR. ALLAN KNIGHT CHALMERS

of Boston University—National Treasurer, N.A.A.C.P.
Back from repeated visits to Alabama and Mississippi.

MR. EDWARD L. COOPER

Executive Secretary, Boston Branch, N.A.A.C.P.

JUDGE LAWRENCE G. BROOKS, Chairman

Question Period

FRIDAY, MAY 4, 1956, 8:00 P.M.

QUINN AUDITORIUM   RINDGE TECH HIGH SCHOOL

BROADWAY and IRVING STREETS   CAMBRIDGE

Sponsored by

American Friends Service Committee   Charles Street Forum on Social Issues

Fellowship of Reconciliation   Women's International League for Peace
and Freedom

National Association for the Advancement of Colored People

Opportunity To Support N. A. A. C. P. — All Are Invited

33

a request to send money to the Montgomery Improvement Association, care of Rev. Dr. Martin Luther King Jr., Dexter Ave. Baptist Church. The triple strategy of informing, recruiting, and fundraising was a formula for using material culture that civil rights organizations often used.[16]

The NAACP continued to press for desegregation throughout 1956 and used mailers [FIGURE 3.20] to raise funds and promote public discussions of its objectives. The NAACP held a meeting at Rindge Tech High School in Cambridge, Massachusetts, on Friday, May 4, 1956, in an attempt to link the struggle in the South with the challenges faced by African Americans in the North. The mailer read, in part:

> "Desegregation and the NAACP"
> What are the conditions in the South today?
> What are the objectives of the NAACP?
> What should "Northerners" do—or not do?

After *Brown*, in the face of tremendous opposition, the NAACP developed a clear strategy for achieving further legal victories. The NAACP's ability to combat segregation was tested when an Alabama judge banned the group from operating in the state just three weeks later, on May 26, 1956. On June 5, 1956, Rev. Fred Shuttlesworth, along with a thousand supporters, formed the Alabama Christian Movement for Human Rights (ACMHR) at Sardis Baptist Church to coordinate boycotts and protests against segregation in Birmingham. The ACMHR also led efforts to integrate schools and raised tens of thousands of dollars for its legal defense fund.[17]

Also on June 5, 1956, a three-judge US District Court panel ruled that Montgomery's bus segregation laws deprived people of equal protection under the Fourteenth Amendment and enjoined Montgomery, along with the rest of Alabama, from enforcing segregated bus travel. After the state and city appealed, the US Supreme Court upheld the

3.20
"Desegregation and the N.A.A.C.P." mailer, 8.5 x 11", 1956

3.21
SCLC "Freedom Now!"
Martin Luther King Jr.
President button with
Observer ribbon,
1.5 x 5.5", 1957

district court ruling on November 13, 1956, ordering Alabama and Montgomery to desegregate their buses. Mayor Gayle was given written notice by federal marshals on December 20, 1956, and the boycott was called off after 381 days.[18]

Even though Rosa Parks was an admirer of Dr. King and is associated with the nonviolent direct-action tactics he championed, she never fully embraced nonviolence and always kept guns to protect herself and her family. She expressed later that after the boycott, she felt ignored by the Movement. Tired of feeling afraid under threats from hostile whites, she and her husband, Raymond, moved to Detroit in 1958, where she soon became a follower of Malcolm X and worked in US Representative John Conyers Jr.'s legislative office. She began to move in Black nationalist circles in Detroit with people who were active in the Dodge Revolutionary Union Movement (DRUM), the Revolutionary Action Movement (RAM), and the Republic of New Africa (RNA) in the mid- to late 1960s. The simplified legend of Rosa Parks presented in items like the comic book *Martin Luther King and the Montgomery Story* became easier to tell than the complicated history of the real person—demonstrating that material culture was capable of impacting not only the results and objectives of the Movement but also the narratives defining it.[19]

The efforts of Rev. Dr. Martin Luther King Jr. in Birmingham and in the Montgomery bus boycott propelled him to national prominence as the leading spokesperson for the growing Civil Rights Movement. King used nonviolent, passive-resistance tactics incorporating peaceful protest, noncooperation, and civil disobedience, which caused many to support the Movement's objectives. King's message resonated with many white Americans, in its blending of American patriotic ideals with the theology of Christian love, but the ongoing violent resistance to desegregation caused many to question these tactics' effectiveness.

In January 1957, at the urging of King, Rev. C. K. Steele, and Rev. Fred Shuttlesworth, Southern Black ministers met at Ebenezer Baptist Church in Atlanta to discuss creating an organization to coordinate future bus boycotts across the South. At a second meeting, the ministers formed the Southern Negro Leaders Conference on Transportation and Nonviolent Integration to focus on bus integration and chose King as president. In August 1957, the group changed its name to the Southern Christian Leadership Conference (SCLC) and decided it would serve as an umbrella organization to combat all forms of segregation. The SCLC worked with the MIA, the ACMHR, the NAACP, and later, CORE and the Student Nonviolent Coordinating Committee (SNCC). The SCLC immediately began to produce items to help them achieve their objectives. The button with ribbon in FIGURE 3.21 belonged to an election observer and was possibly given out at the first SCLC meeting.[20]

The Civil Rights Movement made great strides toward equality in the 1950s, but as segregation and white supremacy was challenged, opposition to desegregation mounted. *Martin Luther King and the Montgomery Story* referred to the "Civil Rights Movement" as a shared national campaign, but the reality was more complex.[21] In September 1957, at the same time that this comic book was being sold across the nation, Arkansas governor Orval Faubus was attempting to prevent nine Black high school students in Little Rock from attending Central High School; President Dwight D. Eisenhower federalized the Arkansas National Guard to allow the students to attend school in the face of violent resistance. Great strides were made, but there was much work to be done. Objects like comics and flyers got the word out, and buttons and pinbacks worn by brave supporters helped organizations raise funds, file lawsuits, increase membership, and find a common purpose.

CHAPTER FOUR

Growing the Movement (1960–1965)

During the 1960s, students took the lead in challenging segregation and disenfranchisement. Long-standing organizations such as the Congress of Racial Equality and the National Association for the Advancement of Colored People (NAACP) worked with student groups such as the Student Nonviolent Coordinating Committee (SNCC) and the Southern Student Organizing Committee (SSOC) to combat Jim Crow. Activists focused their efforts on outlawing segregation, which culminated in the passage of the Civil Rights Act of 1964. Protecting the ballot then became the focus of the efforts of civil rights organizations, resulting in the passage of the Voting Rights Act of 1965.[1]

On February 1, 1960, four students from North Carolina Agricultural and Technical College (Joseph McNeil, Franklin McCain, Ezell Blair Jr., and David Richmond) decided to challenge segregation in Greensboro, North Carolina, by remaining seated at F. W. Woolworth's lunch counter until they were given service. The men, later known as the Greensboro

OPPOSITE
Twelve-year-old Edith Lee Payne holding a pennant at the March on Washington for Jobs and Freedom, August 28, 1963

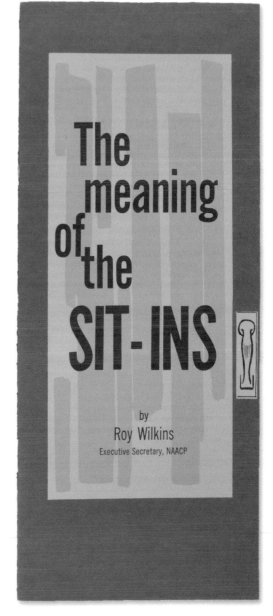

The meaning of the SIT-INS

by
Roy Wilkins
Executive Secretary, NAACP

4.1 (BOTTOM LEFT)
**Student Nonviolent
Coordinating Committee
"We Shall Overcome" button,
2.25", 1960**
4.2 (TOP LEFT)
**CORE "Support Sit-Ins"
pinback, 1.5", 1960**
4.3 (RIGHT)
**NAACP, "The Meaning of the
Sit-Ins" pamphlet, 4 x 9", 1960**

Four, returned the next day and were denied service again, but they continued to return despite being bullied, jailed, and beaten. The sustained sit-ins at the Greensboro Woolworth's caused sales to drop by a third, and the store's management decided to desegregate the lunch counter by asking Black employees Charles Bess, Mattie Long, Susie Morrison, and Jamie Robinson to take a seat at the counter and order a meal on July 25, 1960.[2] During the nearly six months of the sit-ins, objects such as pamphlets and buttons were used to show support for the protestors, to raise funds for civil rights organizations (CORE and SNCC), and to cultivate the growing sense of a national Civil Rights Movement.

For several years after the lunch counter in Greensboro was desegregated, civil rights activists staged sit-ins in dozens of cities to push for integration.[3] The SNCC was founded on April 17, 1960, at Shaw University in Raleigh, North Carolina, by students who emerged as leaders of the sit-in movement. Ella Baker aided young people in forming a locally based, student-run organization. SNCC, along with the Congress of Racial Equality (CORE), helped organize the Greensboro sit-ins and trained hundreds to use the tactic of sit-ins in protests across the country.[4]

Objects such as the iconic "We Shall Overcome" button [FIGURE 4.1] helped SNCC activists spread the word about the sit-ins, recruit new members into SNCC, and raise much-needed funds for the new organization. SNCC was not alone in their use of material culture to further its objectives. Long-standing civil rights organizations such as CORE and the NAACP also participated in sit-in protests. SNCC and CORE worked with the NAACP, which provided funding and organizational support as well as pinbacks, buttons, and pamphlets, to educate the public about the purpose of the sit-ins. The sale of buttons and pinbacks, such as the one stating "Support Sit-Ins / CORE" in FIGURE 4.2 helped the organizations continue their efforts, and the people who chose to wear them showed their support for the Movement's objectives.

NAACP Executive Secretary Roy Wilkins wrote "The Meaning of the Sit-Ins" pamphlet [FIGURE 4.3] in September 1960 to raise awareness of nonviolent direct action as a tactic against segregation. The contents of the pamphlet were based on a speech given by Secretary Wilkins at the City Club forum of Cleveland, Ohio, on April 16, 1960. Wilkins notes that the tactic of nonviolent protest was spreading across the country to challenge segregated facilities:

> Since February 1, 1960, the so-called race problem has taken a fresh and dramatic turn. Beginning on that date in Greensboro, N.C., a wave of sit-ins by Negro college students at lunch counters of variety stores has swept across the South, from Florida to West Texas.

The pamphlet provides several vignettes from around the country in which sit-ins were used to challenge segregation ordinances and links them as a single growing freedom movement at home and abroad. Wilkins notes the grassroots nature of the sit-in protests, stating, "This is the *real* United States underneath the mask which cowardly, cruel, crafty and greedy men have sought to hold in place." It spreads the word about the goals of the sit-ins: to end segregated public facilities, increase a sense of a united national campaign, and boost recruitment and funding levels for varied civil rights organizations such as the NAACP, CORE, and SNCC.[5]

By the end of the summer of 1960, more than seventy-thousand people nationwide had participated in sit-in protests. The slow process of desegregation became a growing national movement by the end of 1960, as thousands of public facilities were integrated. Civil rights organizations produced publications and mailers—these nonviolent weapons—to challenge segregation and to press for integration through legislation, as well as in practice. Mailers such as the one in FIGURES 4.4 + 4.4A, created by CORE, encouraged supporters to take "A Pledge" not to shop in F. W. Woolworth

4.4
CORE pledge card mailer (front), 5 x 3", 1960

4.4A
CORE pledge card mailer (reverse), 5 x 3", 1960

stores until they were fully integrated across the country. The campaign led to many joining CORE, paying their dues, and supporting the organization's operations. Printed matter like this enabled CORE and other civil rights organizations to spread the word, raise funds, recruit members, and advance the national policy goal of desegregation.

The Committee to Defend Martin Luther King Jr. began in 1960 to fund King's defense against felony charges of perjury for allegedly filing fraudulent tax returns. The committee was chaired by A. Philip Randolph and raised money for King's legal defense, voter registration drives, and student-led protests such as sit-ins. The sale of buttons

[FIGURE 4.5] supported the committee's efforts on behalf of King, who was later acquitted by an all-white jury in Alabama, and wearing one demonstrated solidarity with the growing movement to combat Jim Crow nationally.

Continuing the tactic of nonviolent direct action, members of CORE intended to test whether the Supreme Court's ruling in *Boynton v. Virginia* (1960), which declared segregation on interstate bus and rail stations unconstitutional, was being enforced. Members of CORE departed from Washington, DC, on May 4, 1961, planning to travel to New Orleans and challenge segregation laws as they made stops throughout the South.

These Freedom Riders, as they were called, were immediately met with violent resistance, but they persevered.[6] They were attacked in Charlotte, North Carolina, and Rock Hill, South Carolina. And after they met with King in Atlanta, one of their buses was firebombed in the town of Anniston, Alabama. A second bus made it to Birmingham, where many Freedom Riders were beaten by members of the Ku Klux Klan aided by local police. The riders were forced to travel to

4.5 (ABOVE LEFT)
Committee to Defend Martin Luther King Jr. "Support Student Sit-Ins" button, 2", 1960
4.6 (ABOVE RIGHT)
CORE "Freedom Ride" pinback, 1.5", 1961

New Orleans by plane, under federal protection, due to the threat to their lives, but other student-led organizations, such as the Nashville Student Movement, began their own freedom rides throughout the South.[7]

Federal troops were dispatched to protect the Nashville riders inside the First Baptist Church in Montgomery, Alabama, from an angry white mob; once the riders entered Mississippi, they were arrested. Students and other activists continued to descend on Jackson, Mississippi, throughout the summer of 1961. The national attention caused President John F. Kennedy to announce that he would direct the Interstate Commerce Commission to outlaw segregation in facilities under its jurisdiction. The Freedom Riders continued through November, until the ban took effect, and demonstrated that that tactic of nonviolent direct action worked.[8]

Material culture was critical to organizing the Freedom Rides and in publicizing the ongoing segregation in transportation. Objects such as buttons and pinbacks had an impact, when displayed in public, on those who wore them and saw them. Freedom Riders and their supporters wore buttons such as this Freedom Riders CORE pinback [FIGURE 4.6] and Freedom Now pinback with a ribbon [FIGURE 4.7] as a show of solidarity and to express their support for integration.

Despite some gains made toward desegregation, resistance to integration intensified and white supremacists continued to use violence to maintain the system of segregation. On November 17, 1961, in Albany, Georgia, members of SNCC and the NAACP began the Albany Movement, which sought to end segregation in the city through nonviolent direct action. African Americans occupied bus stations, libraries, and lunch counters, launched boycotts, and marched on City Hall in an effort to force the city to integrate. The activists were met with vehement opposition.[9]

The arrival of King caused the protests to gain national attention, but violence and mass arrests made it harder to find volunteers and derailed the Albany Movement. King was

4.7 (ABOVE)
CORE "Freedom Now" pinback with ribbon, 1.25 x 5.5", 1963

arrested with Ralph Abernathy and other demonstrators for marching on a sidewalk without a permit. King and Abernathy each elected to serve their term rather than pay the fine but were released after an unidentified man paid their bail. They were arrested again for the same offense and ordered to leave Albany, where public facilities remained segregated. After mixed results in Albany, organizations such as the Southern Christian Leadership Conference (SCLC) moved their desegregation efforts to Birmingham and Montgomery, where white supremacists again resorted to violence against civil rights demonstrators.[10]

The Freedom Singers, a vocal quartet from Albany, Georgia, began touring the country in 1960 to raise money for SNCC [FIGURES 4.8 + 4.8A]. They returned to Albany to participate in desegregation efforts by performing freedom songs at meetings and demonstrations. The lyrics of gospel songs such as "This Little Light of Mine" and "Trouble in the Air" were sung and adapted to the freedom struggle. Instead of the lyrics "Over my head I see trouble in the air," Freedom Singer Dr. Bernice Reagon, by her account, changed the wording almost spontaneously to "Over my head I see freedom in the air." She recounted that there was a tremendous reaction from the crowd, and the Freedom Singers continued to perform the song with the updated lyrics. Many of these renditions became the iconic anthems of the Civil Rights Movement.[11]

The Student Nonviolent Coordinating Committee produced the album *Freedom in the Air: A Documentary on Albany, Georgia, 1961–1962* [FIGURE 4.9] to promote awareness of the Albany Movement, recruit members, and raise money for the new organization. The recording, produced by Alan Lomax and Guy Carawan, features a striking 1961 image of protestors kneeling on a sidewalk in Albany, Georgia, on the cover. The original price was $3.98 and came with a subscription to SNCC's publication, the *Student Voice*. Those who purchased the item often displayed the album

4.8 (OPPOSITE TOP)
"SNCC Freedom Singers"
pamphlet (front),
8.5 x 3.5", 1964
4.8A (OPPOSITE BOTTOM LEFT)
"SNCC Freedom Singers"
pamphlet (reverse),
8.5 x 3.5", 1964
4.9 (OPPOSITE BOTTOM RIGHT)
SNCC *Freedom in the Air:*
A Documentary on Albany,
***Georgia* album, 12.25 x 12.25",**
1961/1962

The Songs of the Freedom Singers

The songs of the Freedom Singers come from the country churches, the stockades, the prisons, the farmers' shacks, and the dusty roads of the South. They cry out from the freedom rallies, the picket lines, the crowded cells, the sit-in demonstrations, and the voter registration drives that bring hope to people and an area once without hope. They protest white-only restaurants and hotels, voter discrimination, economic pressures and deprivation, and intimidation and brutality by white citizens and police . . . and they strengthen the spirit and drive that is changing all this. Like the civil rights workers themselves, these songs are bringing justice and freedom to the South. Without them, the movement would lack a vital and enriching force which brings depth and meaning to the cry for Freedom Now.

Student Nonviolent Coordinating Committee
6 Raymond Street, N. W.
Atlanta, Georgia 30314

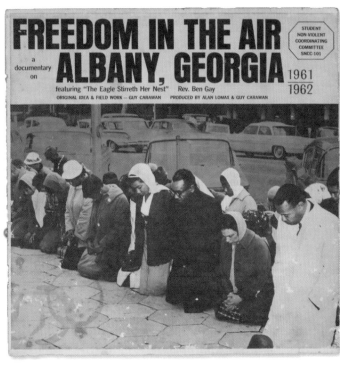

4.10 (TOP RIGHT)
75th Anniversary of the Founding of Mound Bayou, Mississippi, pinback, 1.75", 1962
4.11 (TOP LEFT)
"Never" pinback (worn upside down), .75", 1963
4.12 (BOTTOM LEFT)
"Never" pinback (worn upside down), 1", 1963
4.13 (BOTTOM RIGHT)
"Evers in Memoriam Freedom" pinback, 1", 1963

cover to spark discussion and to show their support for SNCC's fight against segregation. The sales helped finance SNCC's numerous efforts around the country.[12]

The town of Mound Bayou, Mississippi, celebrated its seventy-fifth anniversary on July 12, 1962. The town was founded in 1887 by the formerly enslaved Isaiah T. Montgomery and his cousin Benjamin T. Green to serve as a safer place for African Americans to raise families and distance themselves from Jim Crow. In 1952, budding civil rights activist Medgar Evers moved to Mound Bayou, where he met Dr. T. R. M. Howard, who introduced Evers to the Regional Council of Negro Leadership (RCNL). RCNL organized protests criticizing the FBI's handling of Emmett Till's murder investigation and the acquittal of Till's killers.[13]

The pinback in FIGURE 4.10 commemorates the founding of Mound Bayou and features portraits of its founders. This pinback not only served as a proud reminder of the city's origins but also made a powerful public statement about the residents' resistance to Jim Crow. Mound Bayou became a symbol of the impact of segregation on the lives of African Americans around the country. Wearing this pinback empowered the people of Mound Bayou to continue their city's legacy of opposing segregation while showing resolve to those who fought against their civil rights.

Despite some success of nonviolent direct action to confront segregation—and probably because of it—white supremacists wore "never" pinbacks to show their opposition to integration [FIGURES 4.11 + 4.12]. Civil rights activists wore those pinbacks upside down to demonstrate their support for the growing Civil Rights Movement and the constitutional right of all Americans to equal protection under the law.[14]

In June 1963, Alabama governor George C. Wallace stood in the doorway of the University of Alabama's enrollment office, preventing two Black students from entering, and on June 10, President Kennedy federalized the Alabama National Guard to protect the students. The efforts of activists, as well as the public's growing support for protecting civil rights, convinced Kennedy to give a speech on June 11, 1963, that was broadcast on radio and television, supporting the integration of the University of Alabama and the passage of the Civil Rights Act. The law, if passed, would outlaw discrimination based on "race" and "color," effectively making segregation illegal at the federal level.

On June 12, just hours after President Kennedy's speech, Medgar Evers was assassinated in front of his home in Jackson, Mississippi, by Klansman Byron De La Beckwith.

Evers had a long record of peaceful opposition to Jim Crow; his assassination was an immediate reaction to what segregationists saw as an end to generations of white-only rule.[15] The shooting was part of a coordinated plan to murder civil rights activists in locations across three states, including Selma, Alabama, and sites throughout Louisiana. Despite De La Beckwith's fingerprints being found on the rifle used to murder Evers and his boasts about the crime to members of the White Citizens' Council, an all-white jury acquitted him. De La Beckwith was retried and convicted in 1994 and died in prison in 2001. When he was shot, Medgar Evers was carrying NAACP T-shirts he had retrieved from the trunk of his car.[16]

The pinback in FIGURE 4.13 was produced soon after to honor Evers's life and legacy as a dedicated foot soldier for equality. The black-and-white button states, "Evers / In Memoriam / freedom." This powerful message helped those involved in the freedom struggle to persevere through this difficult moment. It was a signal to supporters to continue the fight against segregation and a signal to white supremacists that violence would not stop the Movement's momentum.

The United Freedom Movement (UFM) formed June 3, 1963, in Cleveland, Ohio, as a way to bring together long-standing civil rights, civic, and fraternal organizations such as CORE and the NAACP with organizations in Cleveland that wanted to use direct action. The groups agreed on a platform focused on voting, running for office, education, health, and jobs. To achieve these goals, they decided that they would negotiate with local and state officials, but if their demands were not met, they would use direct action—a strategy the UFM began to employ in June and July of 1963, when it threatened to picket over hiring discrimination.[17]

The NAACP and CORE organized a March for Freedom in Cleveland on July 14, 1963. About twenty thousand people marched to Cleveland Stadium to rally in support of the objectives of the UFM. Among the speakers were the NAACP's national executive secretary, Roy Wilkins, and

4.14
March for Freedom
flyer, 6 x 9", 1963

All Citizens of Cleveland

JOIN IN THE UNITED FREEDOM MOVEMENT

March for Freedom

SUN., JULY 14th, 1963

Get in step with the

FIGHT FOR ALL CIVIL RIGHTS

MARCH TO CLEVELAND STADIUM

HEAR

ROY WILKINS, National Executive Secretary
NAACP.

JAMES FARMER, National Executive Director
CORE

MAKE THIS A DAY TO REMEMBER

Parade Assembly Point

24th & Chester   13th & Chester

3:00 P. M.

PUBLIC INVITED

FOOD CONCESSIONS WILL BE OPEN IN THE STADIUM

GENERAL CHAIRMEN;
REV. SUMPTER RILEY, CHAS. P. LUCAS, REV. LEROY KELLEY

Progressive Printing Co.   112

CORE's national executive director, James Farmer. Printed pieces such as the flyer in FIGURE 4.14 enabled UFM to quickly mobilize thousands of people in a way that word of mouth could not do.[18]

The UFM decided to focus on education in 1964 and charged the Cleveland school system with widespread segregation. It led sit-ins at the school board building in February and a school boycott in April. In 1965, the UFM backed the candidacy of Carl Stokes, who lost to the incumbent, Mayor Ralph Locher. Two years later, in 1967, Stokes defeated Locher in the Democratic primary and Republican Seth Taft in the general election, becoming the first Black mayor of a large American city.[19]

In late 1962, A. Philip Randolph, president of the Brotherhood of Sleeping Car Porters, had asked Bayard Rustin to begin planning a march on Washington, DC. Randolph had planned a march during World War II to protest segregation in the armed forces and discrimination in the defense industry. That march was called off in 1941 in exchange for President Roosevelt's issuing of Executive Order 8802, which banned racial discrimination in the defense industry (later the basis for the Fair Employment Act, discussed in Chapter Two). Leaders from many civil rights organizations decided that a march on Washington was necessary to force the federal government to take action on civil rights. Organizations and individuals disagreed about the purpose of the march, but it became a watershed moment in the Civil Rights Movement. March organizers, including Randolph and SCLC President King, reached compromise, if not consensus, with the leaders of student organizations like SNCC in an effort to demonstrate widespread support for the civil rights bill, which had been languishing in the halls of Congress.[20]

While the march was being planned, events across the country contributed to a mounting sense of frustration at the lack of progress on a bill that would outlaw segregation and various other forms of discrimination on a national scale. Americans saw the violent images from the Birmingham demonstrations in the spring of 1963, which increased pressure on the Kennedy administration to support the civil rights bill. On June 11, 1963, the day that Kennedy gave his speech in support of equal civil rights, voting rights, and desegregation, leaders of the SCLC expressed their plans to organize the massive march on Washington, DC, to show support for the passage of federal civil rights protections.[21]

On June 22, President Kennedy met with the "Big Six," the leaders of the most prominent civil rights organizations in the country: Randolph; King; James Farmer, national director of CORE; Roy Wilkins, executive director of the NAACP; John Lewis, chairman of SNCC; and Whitney Young, executive director of the Urban League. Kennedy hoped he could convince them to call off the march, but they refused, and on July 2, 1963, Randolph and King gathered the Big Six to discuss the march's purpose, planning, and tactics.[22]

The effort was Herculean—logistically and financially and also in terms of reaching a consensus about the objectives of the march and the content of the speeches. The Urban League and the NAACP wanted it to focus on the proposed civil rights bill, believing that adding other causes would dilute the march's political impact. SNCC and CORE believed that it was critical for the agenda to address economic discrimination, unemployment, and low wages. Randolph wanted the march to focus on jobs and economic progress; King wanted to emphasize civil rights.

The Big Six decided to make the march about "jobs and freedom," but there were further disagreements about the tactics to be used on the day of the march. King and the SCLC wanted the march to include sit-ins at government buildings, but the NAACP and Urban League opposed direct action because they believed it would prevent President Kennedy from conceding to their demands.[23] Student-led organizations such as SNCC were furious when it was decided that there would be no direct action in Washington. SNCC wanted to apply as much pressure as possible to hasten federal action on civil rights. Lewis also wanted the content of the speeches to take a more forceful tone and the scope of the march to be broadened to include police brutality and voter suppression.[24]

Conspicuously absent from both the initial planning sessions and the speaking roster were Black women—despite the fact that they were integral to the grassroots efforts of each of the organizations. This reflected the misogyny that was still very prevalent in most organizations of the day. Although women were not involved in the conceptual planning of the march, they were involved in intermediate planning stages to organize the logistics.[25]

Betty Holton was a field secretary at the Washington, DC, headquarters of the NAACP. She was pictured in a July 1963 United Press International photograph passing out some of the thousands of March on Washington pinbacks sold and distributed before, during and after the march. In her hands are some of the thousands of buttons sold and distributed before, during, and after the march. Holton continued her involvement in the Movement, becoming a delegate to the National Nominating Committee in 1967, campaign chair for Washington, DC, in 1970, and then president of the Washington, DC, chapter and a member of the NAACP National Board.[26]

The Big Six worked through their differences and developed "ten demands," which King announced as part of his famed "I Have a Dream" speech on the National Mall, asking the crowd to affirm. The ten demands reflected the organizations' various goals. Organizers knew that this moment could become a catalyst for sweeping political change and that the Movement's objectives had to be clear:

1. Comprehensive and effective *civil rights legislation* from the present Congress—without compromise or filibuster—to guarantee all Americans access to all public

accommodations, decent housing, adequate and integrated education, the right to vote.

2. Withholding of Federal funds from all programs in which discrimination exists.

3. *Desegregation of all school districts in 1963.*

4. Enforcement of the *Fourteenth Amendment*—reducing Congressional representation of states where citizens are disfranchised.

5. A new *Executive Order* banning discrimination in all housing supported by federal funds.

6. Authority for the Attorney General to institute *injunctive suits* when any constitutional right is violated.

7. A massive federal program to train and place all unemployed workers—Negro and white—on meaningful and dignified jobs at decent wages.

8. A national *minimum* wage act that will give all Americans a decent standard of living. (Government surveys show that anything less than $2.00 an hour fails to do this.)

9. A broadened *Fair Labor Standards Act* to include all areas of employment which are presently excluded.

10. A federal *Fair Employment Practices Act* barring discrimination by federal, state and municipal governments, and by employers, contractors, employment agencies, and trade unions.

While the demands were set, the content of the speeches was in flux up to the day of the march. John Lewis—the youngest speaker that day—wanted to challenge the Kennedy administration to do far more, including addressing police brutality. Lewis agreed to remove some language that might be seen as too embarrassing or radical for the administration, but he still wanted to deliver a speech that "had bite."[27]

March organizers were well prepared for the large numbers of peaceful marchers expected to participate, and they were also prepared with thousands of objects that, when worn or displayed, would express to the millions watching around the world the objectives of the massive demonstration. Marchers and organizers understood the importance of using the march to achieve as many goals of the freedom movement as possible. Bringing hundreds of thousands of people together in the nation's capital was not merely a symbolic act. Those in the Movement understood that they had to use this event as a catalyst for sweeping legislative reform.

Organizers used flyers, buttons, pinbacks, and posters to promote the march and to encourage people to attend. Cleveland Robinson, chairman of the administrative committee, and Bayard Rustin, deputy director, paid for the printing and distribution of thousands of flyers, which were passed out and posted in the weeks leading up to August 28, 1963. The flyer in FIGURE 4.15 was union made in New York. Although it was meant to be discarded, when participants brought it home, it served as a tool to educate many more people about the civil rights bill, as well as the economic goals of the march.

Rustin, along with his chief of staff, Tom Kahn, ran the daily operations for the march from the Harlem headquarters listed on the flyer. Each sponsoring organization contributed financially and sent a representative to work in the headquarters. CORE sent Norman Hill and Blyden Jackson, while SNCC sent Courtland Cox and Joyce and Dorie Ladner.

Part of the operating budget was earmarked for producing promotional items. The sale of those buttons, pinbacks, and posters helped to raise further organizing funds, as well as to pay for the buses that brought supporters from around the country—particularly the deep South—to Washington, DC. The Workers Defense League tasked Rachelle Horowitz with coordinating these busing efforts. The NAACP, CORE, and SNCC, as well as smaller student groups, religious groups, and labor unions, chartered buses that transported thousands of people.[28]

Those who traveled from the West Coast left days before August 28, and many of those farther east gathered together

4.15
March on Washington flyer, 5.5 x 8.25", 1963

110

Mathew Ahmann
Eugene Carson Blake
James Farmer
Martin Luther King, Jr.
John Lewis

Joachim Prinz
A. Philip Randolph
Walter Reuther
Roy Wilkins
Whitney Young

Appeal to you to

MARCH on
WASHINGTON

WEDNESDAY, AUGUST 28, 1963

We Demand:
— Meaningful Civil Rights Legislation
— Massive Federal Works Program
— Full and Fair Employment

— Decent Housing
— The Right to Vote
— Adequate Integrated Education

FOR BUS RESERVATIONS CALL:

BROOKLYN — UL 7-9200 or HY 3-1671

BRONX — FA 4-5819 or DA 3-8060

MANHATTAN — MO 6-0401

National Office

MARCH ON WASHINGTON
FOR JOBS AND FREEDOM

170 West 130 Street   •   New York 27, N.Y.   •   FI 8-1900

Cleveland Robinson
Chairman, Administrative Committee

Bayard Rustin
Deputy Director

4.16 (ABOVE)
Participants in the March on Washington, August 28, 1963

4.16 (ABOVE)
Participants in the March on Washington, August 28, 1963
4.17 (OPPOSITE LEFT)
"March on Washington for Jobs and Freedom" button, 2.25", 1963
4.18 (OPPOSITE RIGHT)
August 28 "March on Washington for Jobs and Freedom" button, 1.75", 1963

before boarding buses and trains or driving caravans of cars. People gathered in Kelly Ingram Park in Birmingham, Alabama, where demonstrators faced dogs and fire hoses across from the Sixteenth Street Baptist Church before heading to DC. In Greensboro and Durham, North Carolina, marchers coordinated hundreds to leave by car, and a twenty-two-car "Freedom Special" train picked up marchers on its way up the East Coast.[29]

Wherever the marchers came from and however they got there, the mood on the morning of the march was a jubilant feeling of unity. Tens of thousands of marchers began forming at the Washington Monument on the morning of August 28, 1963, while the Big Six were meeting with members of Congress to press for meaningful legislation. The marchers began to sing freedom songs and headed down Independence and Constitution Avenues toward the Lincoln Memorial around 11:30 a.m. Thousands more arrived throughout the day, and more than 250,000 marched and listened to the speeches [FIGURE 4.16].

Tens of thousands of those marchers wore buttons, pinbacks, and hats. They held signs and posters and passed out flyers to show their support for the objectives of the Civil Rights Movement. The most recognizable artifact from the march is a 2.25-inch button that featured Black and white hands shaking [FIGURE 4.17], which was distributed in the thousands by march organizers. This image can be traced back to the earliest mutual aid societies started by African Americans in the late nineteenth century. The button states, "March on Washington for Jobs & Freedom / August 28, 1963," with a union bug above the date. There were several other buttons made for the march, including a smaller version that measures 1.75 inches [FIGURE 4.18], which includes the month and day but not the year, and a larger 3.5-inch version of the 2.25-inch button that was manufactured on a smaller scale. Thousands of additional buttons were made referring to it as the "March for Freedom," stating, "I Was There, August 28, 1963." John Lewis recalled that the buttons were "everywhere that day in Washington," as they were at every major civil rights demonstration of the early 1960s.[30]

The 2.25-inch button was present at the most iconic and lasting moment of the day: the "I Have a Dream" speech given by King. He wore the button on his upper left lapel, making it easy to see and prominent in virtually every photograph and moving image taken of the speech. That moment imbued that object with a certain significance that would, from that moment on, resonate with anyone who wore it or saw it being worn.

King's speech before hundreds of thousands stirred all those who heard it; it has become the lasting symbol of the March on Washington. King spoke about how the nation needed to live up to its own ideals of equality under the law and justice without prejudice.

Several others spoke after King, including Randolph and Rustin, who read the ten demands, and the march ended with the crowd joining hands and singing "We Shall Overcome." As the marchers dispersed, members of SNCC gathered, formed a circle, and continued to sing. Coordinating the march had been a huge accomplishment, but they knew that larger struggles lay ahead. They were gathering strength for that long fight, aware that they had helped to spread seeds that would take root across the country.

At the same time, media coverage of the event was widespread and generally positive; for many Americans, it was the first civil rights demonstration they had witnessed. Countless photographs ran in newspapers and were broadcast around the world, and signs, buttons, hats, banners, posters, and flyers are present in nearly every photograph taken that day.[31] Those objects, like all the material culture of the Civil Rights Movement, encouraged people to ask questions, get involved, donate to civil rights organizations, and put pressure on members of Congress to pass a civil rights bill.

The March on Washington was deeply meaningful to those who participated, and it solidified a growing sense that the Civil Rights Movement was gaining momentum. It focused the world's attention on the persistence of Jim

4.19
"A Strong Civil Rights Bill by Christmas!" pamphlet, 4 x 9", 1963

call for
a national campaign for

A STRONG CIVIL RIGHTS BILL

BY CHRISTMAS!

The Civil Rights Bill before Congress is in danger. There is a concerted effort to water down the bill in the interest of political expediency—in the belief that the Negro's appetite for freedom can be satisfied by a half-way measure.

Yet the need for strong civil rights legislation grows more urgent every day. In the South, Negro demonstrators are the victims of incredible police brutality. They desperately need the protection that Part III of the Civil Rights Bill can provide. This would enable the Attorney General to take injunctive action against fire hoses and police dogs, and to sue violators of our constitutional rights.

Throughout the country Negroes confront a deepening economic crisis as unemployment mounts. We therefore desperately need a Federal Fair Employment Practices Act (FEPC) if the gap between black and white workers is to be closed.

Despite these facts, powerful forces are working to dilute the Civil Rights Bill. Part III and the FEPC are prime targets. No wonder, for these measures were included in the bill after the March on Washington demanded them.

But we demanded more. A quarter million Americans, black and white, told Congress what we wanted on August 28th. You thundered your assent to the demand for:

Comprehensive and effective civil rights legislation from the present Congress — without compromise or filibuster — to guarantee all Americans
 . . . access to all public accommodations
 . . . decent housing
 . . . adequate and integrated education
 . . . the right to vote

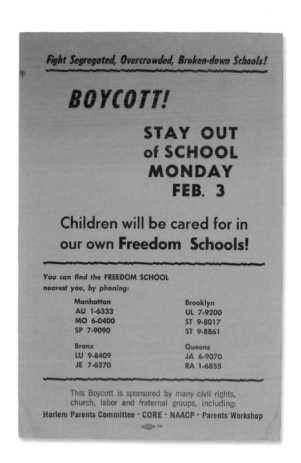

FIG. 4.20 (BOTTOM LEFT)
"Freedom Day February 3 No School" pinback, 1.25", 1964
FIG. 4.21 (TOP LEFT)
"Freedom Stay-Out Better Schools Integrated Schools" pinback, 1.25", 1964
FIG. 4.22 (RIGHT)
"Stay Out of School Monday Feb. 3" flyer, 5.25 x 8.25", 1964
FIG. 4.23 (MIDDLE)
CORE-NAACP "March for Democratic Schools May 18" pinback, 1.25", 1964

Crow in the United States, but even so, the passage of a civil rights bill was not assured, especially after the assassination of President John F. Kennedy on November 22, 1963. Civil rights organizations including CORE, the NAACP, the Allied Organization for Civil Rights, and the Southern Student Organizing Committee pressed for the passage of the Civil Rights Act and an end to segregation.

The Leadership Conference on Civil Rights (a lobbying organization founded in 1950 by Randoph, Wilkins, and Arnold Aronson, director of the National Jewish Community Relations Advisory Council) and the organizers of the March on Washington for Jobs and Freedom called for a national campaign following the march to support the passage of a civil rights bill, as well as a permanent Federal Fair Employment Practices Act. They produced the pamphlet in **FIGURE 4.19** to remind the public about the demands of the march, particularly the passage of a civil rights bill. It was published in October 1963, the month after four girls were killed when Ku Klux Klan members bombed the Sixteenth Street Baptist Church in Birmingham, Alabama. The brutal violence was in stark contrast to the tactics of the peaceful marchers. The pamphlet gave strategies on how to organize at the local level, as well as "The Continuation of Mass Action" across the country. To reinforce these goals, it provided a pledge of support on the reverse:

> When we marched on Washington on August 28th, we did more than make demands. At the Lincoln Memorial we pledged to back up those demands with action! We said:
>
> I pledge that I will join and support all actions undertaken in good faith in accord with the time-honored democratic tradition of nonviolent protest, of peaceful assembly and petition, and of redress through the courts and the legislative process.
>
> We must demand...
> A strong Civil Rights Bill by Christmas!

The pamphlet was distributed only weeks after the March on Washington, capitalizing on the attention it brought to their cause, but it took almost another year of campaigning before the Civil Rights Act passed in July 1964. Material culture such as this pamphlet played a significant role in the eventual passage of the bill, as well as continued efforts at desegregation across the United States.[32]

While those efforts persisted, on February 3, 1964, hundreds of thousands of parents, students, and civil rights activists took part in a citywide boycott of the New York City public school system to demonstrate their support for the full integration and improvement of the city's schools.

Organizers established temporary Freedom Schools in Manhattan, Brooklyn, the Bronx, and Queens to allow children to participate in the protests and still attend school. They were organized by CORE, Harlem Parents Committee, Parents' Workshop for Equality, and the NAACP. Several pinbacks were produced to inform the public about the proposed stay-out and to put pressure on politicians to increase school integration. Each union-made pinback measures 1.25 inches, reading "Freedom Day / Feb. 3 / No School" and "Better Schools / Freedom Stay-Out / Integrated Schools" [FIGURES 4.20 + 4.21]. These buttons continued to be worn afterward to show continued support for integration.[33]

The flyer in FIGURE 4.22 was distributed to promote the stay-out and to provide a practical model for parents to guide their children that morning. It provided the phone numbers of Freedom Schools across the city and listed the boycott's sponsors. Organizers understood that objects such as these flyers were recruitment tools to gain new members, which they would need to continue the nationwide struggle against segregation and racial discrimination.

More than 450,000 students refused to attend school on February 3, but despite the protest's overwhelming support, the city's school board refused to make significant reforms. In Boston, on February 26, 1964, students staged a similar protest to push for integration and better conditions in that city's public schools. The NAACP and CORE produced pinbacks to help spread the word, show support for desegregation, and create a sense of shared struggle [FIGURE 4.23].[34]

On March 5, 1964, the Allied Organization for Civil Rights (AOCR), a regional civil rights organization whose leadership included Frank Stanley Jr., editor of the *Louisville Defender*; Dr. Olof Anderson, synod executive of the Presbyterian Church; and Georgia Davis Powers, who in 1967 became the first African American woman to be elected to the Kentucky State Senate, sponsored the March on Frankfort, Kentucky. The ten thousand people in attendance listened to baseball

4.24
**March on Frankfort
program, 8.5 x 11", 1964**

SOUVENIR PROGRAM

March on Frankfort

REV. DR. MARTIN LUTHER KING, JR.

Thursday, March 5th
1 9 6 4

25c

legend Jackie Robinson and other speakers, including Rev. Ralph Abernathy and Rev. Dr. Martin Luther King Jr. King spoke of the need for a civil rights bill prohibiting segregation and discrimination in public accommodations. The Mammoth Life and Accident Insurance Company produced the program in FIGURE 4.24 as a form of advertising; it cost twenty-five cents and features a photograph of King.[35] The program includes an itinerary of the speakers and text describing the purpose of the March on Frankfort, as well a list of suggestions for "What to Do After the March":

> Write Your Legislator
>
> Support A.O.C.R.
>
> Contact Your Legislator
>
> Talk About Public Accommodations
>
> Call Your Legislator
>
> Come Back to Frankfort
>
> Visit Your Legislator
>
> Work with A.O.C.R.
>
> See Your Legislator.
>
> Until a Good Public Accommodations Bill Is Passed in Kentucky.

The march did not immediately lead to the passage of a civil rights bill in Kentucky, but the national attention it received raised awareness about the federal civil rights bill still in Congress.[36]

The Southern Student Organizing Committee (SSOC) was founded on April 4, 1964, in Nashville, Tennessee. Most of its members were white, which reflected a growing trend of Southern whites beginning to support the Civil Rights Movement because of the violence they witnessed on television and newspapers, as well as firsthand. Many members of SSOC were veterans of the sit-ins or Freedom Rides and were members of organizations like SNCC and CORE.[37]

FIG. 4.25 (TOP)
SSOC "Mobilize the South" pinback, 1.25", 1964
FIG. 4.26 (BOTTOM)
SSOC pinback, 1.25", 1964

The SSOC began producing promotional items after its founding meeting in Nashville, creating striking designs that incorporated and reinterpreted the Confederate battle flag. This powerful symbolism sent a bold message of defiance to supporters of Jim Crow. One pinback reads, "Mobilize the South / SSOC," with the stars and bars of the Confederate flag turned into a peace symbol [FIGURE 4.25]. Another pinback displays an interracial handshake across the symbol of the Old South [FIGURE 4.26]. Both measure 1.25 inches and were union made.

The SSOC produced a pamphlet that commemorated its founding meeting and announced its platform [FIGURES 4.27 + 4.27A]. Its back cover quotes from the preamble of the SSOC Constitution: the "SSOC believes that the South has special problems which create difficulties—and opportunities—for a Southern movement working towards the creation of a new and truly democratic South." Among its top priorities, listed on the pamphlet's flap, was "not only an end to segregation and racism but the rise of full and equal opportunity for all." The SSOC focused on the unique challenges of civil rights activists working in the South and also linked their struggle to the larger goal of federal civil rights legislation.[38]

Efforts across the country were starting to pay off, and members of Congress were feeling increased pressure to pass civil rights legislation. On June 19, 1964, the Civil Rights Act passed the US Senate. To show support, the Coordinating Council of Community Organizations (CCCO) planned a rally two days later in Chicago, on June 21. The CCCO had been involved in the Freedom Stay-Out boycotts in Chicago and was hoping to bring attention to local issues, in addition to demonstrating its support for federal civil rights legislation. The list of speakers for the rally included James Farmer, Rev. Dr. Martin Luther King Jr., and James Forman of SNCC, as well as a performance by the gospel singer Mahalia Jackson. Seventy-five thousand people attended the Illinois Rally for Civil Rights in Chicago's Soldier Field. The rally concluded with the reading of "A Pledge of Action for Civil Rights"—a statement of support for nonviolent demonstrations, civil rights platforms for the Republican and Democratic parties, equality of opportunity, and full integration of Illinois schools. Promotional buttons for the rally read, "Illinois Rally for Civil Rights / I Care / I'll Be There / Soldier Field, June 21, 1964" [FIGURE 4.28]. The buttons were worn prior to the rally and continued to be worn afterward by those who supported the civil rights bill working its way through Congress.[39]

The enormous effort of those involved in the fight against segregation and discrimination in the United States paid off, and the objects used by the organizations, their members, activists, marchers, protestors, and supporters were key to the passage of this landmark piece of legislation. The 1964 Civil Rights Act was enacted on July 2, 1964; it was the most extensive civil rights law passed since Reconstruction. It banned discrimination in employment on the basis of race, color, religion, sex, or national origin and created the Equal Employment Opportunity Commission (EEOC) to investigate and prosecute cases of employment discrimination.[40]

The act also prohibited discrimination in public accommodations, outlawed bias in federally funded programs, provided technical and financial aid for school desegregation, and authorized the US Department of Justice to initiate desegregation lawsuits. Many felt that the Civil Rights Act of 1964 was the high-water mark for the Movement. Through nonviolent action, activists had achieved a major objective of outlawing racial discrimination in the United States, but the process of ending segregation in the United States was far from over.[41]

After the passage of the Civil Rights Act of 1964, activists focused their efforts on enfranchising those whose rights had been systematically denied. Using violence, poll taxes, literacy tests, and other unconstitutional methods, white supremacists had long prevented African Americans from exercising their right to vote. Organizations such as the NAACP, CORE, and

SSOC believes that the South has special problems which create difficulties--and op-portunities--for a Southern movement working towards the creation of a new and truly democratic South. SSOC be-lieves that each individual Southerner must be guaranteed the right to participate in the formulation of the social, economic, and political deci-sions which directly affect his life. SSOC further be-lieves that the South posses-ses valuable traditions, in both black and white cultures, which will enable Southerners to make a unique contribution to a free and democratic America.

--From the Preamble
SSOC Constitution

--/--/--/--/--/--

For more information, sub-scription to The New South Student ($4) and/or membership ($5 - includes subscription) write to the . . .

*Southern Student
Organizing Committee
P. O. Box 6403
Nashville, Tennessee
37212*

4.27 (LEFT)
SSOC "We'll Take Our Stand" pamphlet (front), 4 x 8.75", 1964
4.27A (RIGHT)
SSOC "We'll Take Our Stand" pamphlet (reverse), 4 x 8.75", 1964

SNCC, along with newer organizations such as the Mississippi Freedom Democratic Party, pressed local, state, and national leaders to pass and enforce laws that protected voting rights. These efforts culminated in the passage of the Voting Rights Act of 1965, which provided federal oversight of elections in those states with a history of abusive practices.

Voting rights advocates had led efforts to register African Americans to vote in Mississippi as early as 1952, but they were largely unsuccessful due to the massive resistance and violence used by white supremacists against those seeking to exercise their rights. Rev. George Lee, who served as a vice president of the Regional Council of Negro

Leadership (RCNL), led such an effort. Three weeks after he gave a speech at the RCNL's 1955 annual meeting in Mound Bayou, Mississippi, Lee was shot in the face three times with a shotgun by assailants who pulled up beside him on the highway. The local sheriff ruled his death a traffic accident. Medgar Evers, then a field secretary for the NAACP, continued to try to find Lee's killers but was himself murdered by white supremacist Byron De La Beckwith in June 1963.[42]

Robert "Bob" Moses led SNCC's efforts to register African Americans in Mississippi in 1961, facing tremendous opposition. The Council of Federated Organizations (COFO) was formed in 1962 as a resource for civil rights organizations in their common goal: registering African Americans to vote. COFO consisted of members from SNCC, CORE, and the NAACP. The NAACP provided administrative oversight, CORE directed the voter registration project, and SNCC provided most of the manpower and the funding. Each of these organizations relied on the objects they produced to achieve their objectives.[43]

White supremacists continued to use violence as African Americans pressed the government to protect their voting rights. Numerous acts of violence against African Americans connected to the Movement went unpunished. Herbert Lee, a farmer and charter member of the Amite County, Mississippi, NAACP, was shot by E. H. Hurst, a member of the Mississippi state legislature. Hurst was exonerated, and Louis Allen, a Black witness who later recanted his testimony, was murdered on April 7, 1964. There were numerous other examples of violence committed with impunity against African Americans, with the intent of silencing voting rights campaigns. This, coupled with the scant attention the violence was receiving in the national press, caused civil rights activists in the Deep South to increase their efforts to combat disenfranchisement.[44]

In 1963, Bob Moses, along with Allard Lowenstein, a former dean at Stanford University, organized a "freedom vote"—a mock election that allowed disenfranchised African

4.28 (TOP)
Illinois Rally for Civil Rights button, 2.25", 1964
4.29 (BOTTOM LEFT)
SNCC "One Man One Vote" pinback, 1.25", 1964
4.30 (BOTTOM RIGHT)
FDP "One Man One Vote" pinback, 1.25", 1964

Americans in Mississippi to demonstrate their frustration at not being able to exercise their right to vote. Eighty thousand people voted in that mock election, which convinced Moses and Lowenstein that a larger voter registration effort was possible. In the summer of 1964, volunteers—mostly SNCC members from northern states—registered thousands of African American voters across the Deep South.[45]

Civil rights organizers and the local Black communities debated whether to welcome these young, mostly white volunteers into the Movement. Many prided themselves in their self-reliance and feared that whites would dilute Black control over the direction and tactics of the Movement. This debate was waged throughout 1964 and '65, but activists and Mississippians agreed to work together with the hundreds of

Searching a Mississippi river for bodies of three missing young civil rights workers. Their bodies were later discovered, savagely beaten and bullet-ridden, a black day in the Calendar of Coercion.

Churches Burned, Bombed Or Otherwise Destroyed In Mississippi June 15 through August 14.

JUNE 15: Hattiesburg: Rosary Roman Catholic Church auditorium gutted by fire.

JUNE 15: Philadelphia: Mt. Zion Baptist Church. Bombed. Total loss.

JUNE 21: Brandon, Rankin County: Sweet Rest Church of Christ Holiness. Molotov cocktail. Fire started. Damage not extensive.

JUNE 25: Ruleville: Williams Chapel. Fire bombed. Damage slight. Eight plastic bags of gasoline found later outside building.

JUNE 26: Clinton: Church of Holy Ghost. Arson. Kerosene spilled on floor. Incident occurred after local white pastor spoke to Negro Bible class.

JULY 6: Jackson: McCraven Hill Baptist Church. Kerosene fire. Church has no ties to the civil rights movement.

JULY 6: Raleigh: Local Methodist and Baptist Churches. Burnt to the ground.

JULY 11: Browning: Pleasant Plan Missionary Baptist Church. Burnt to the ground. Whites sought to buy it; Negroes refused to sell.

JULY 12: Natchez: Jerusalem Baptist and Methodist Churches burnt to the ground.

JULY 22: Pike County: Six miles east of Magnolia, Mississippi; near South Entrance of Percy Quinn State Park, four miles from which Mt. Zion was burned June 16. Mt. Vernon Missionary Baptist Church. Leveled by fire.

JULY 24: McComb: Rose Hill Church. Fire. Moderate damage.

JULY 30: Meridian, Mississippi: The Mount Moriah Baptist Church. Totally destroyed by fire.

JULY 31: Brandon: Pleasant Grove Baptist Church burned to the ground. (Located on Highway 80, approximately 3 miles from Brandon.)

AUG. 5: Natchez (Finwick): Mt. Pilgrim Baptist Church. Burned.

AUG. 12: Brandon: St. Matthews Baptist Church. Burned to the ground.

FIG. 4.31 (LEFT)
"Calendar of Coercion"
pamphlet (front), 3.5 x 8",
1964

FIG. 4.31A (RIGHT)
"Calendar of Coercion"
pamphlet (reverse), 3.5 x 8",
1964

volunteers willing to participate in voter registration drives. SNCC leaders decided to focus their efforts on the summer of 1964, with two main goals. The first was to encourage African Americans not to register as part of the Democratic Party, due to their segregationist policies, but instead to support the formation of a new organization, the Mississippi Freedom Democratic Party. The MFDP would send a slate of delegates to the Democratic National Convention in Atlantic City, New Jersey, in August 1964, arguing that they should be seated instead of the delegates from the Mississippi Democratic Party because the new party allowed both Black and white voters to participate. The second goal was to establish Freedom Schools across Mississippi that would teach topics ranging from the Constitution to African American history.[46]

The SNCC produced the "One Man / One Vote" pinback in FIGURE 4.29 for the 1964 voter registration campaigns that became known as Freedom Summer. The MFDP produced a nearly identical pinback in 1964, replacing "SNCC," with "FDP" [FIGURE 4.30]. The sale of this pinback directly funded voter registration efforts in Mississippi as well as the MFDP delegation to the Democratic Convention in August. Pinbacks, as well as banners, posters, and signs produced for the convention, conveyed a message of support for the efforts of Freedom Summer and aided in recruiting new members, as well as generating funds for ongoing efforts in Mississippi and the campaign for passage of legislation to protect voting rights at the federal level.

The Freedom Summer volunteers were immediately met with violence by white locals, the Ku Klux Klan, and the White Citizens' Councils. On June 21, 1964, CORE volunteers James Chaney, Michael Schwerner, and Andrew Goodman were ambushed and murdered by Klansmen after having been arrested, then released from jail by Cecil Price, a Neshoba County, Mississippi, sheriff's deputy and a member of the White Knights of the Ku Klux Klan. When the CORE members went missing, the Council of Federated Organizations

FIG. 4.32 (TOP)
CORE "Black Power" pinback, 1", 1964
FIG. 4.33 (BOTTOM)
SNCC pinback, 1", 1964

pressured the FBI to investigate their disappearance. The FBI resisted until Attorney General Robert F. Kennedy ordered an investigation. On August 4, 1964, the investigation uncovered the bodies of the three slain civil rights activists, as well as the bodies of eight Black men—one of whom was wearing a CORE T-shirt. The murders focused national and international attention on Jim Crow segregation and violence in the South and increased the public's calls for a Voting Rights Act.[47]

CORE played a key role in linking Freedom Summer to the broader national campaign, pressing for legislation that specifically addressed the Jim Crow tactics used by white supremacists. Objects such as the "Calendar of Coercion" pamphlet in **FIGURES 4.31 + 4.31A** were used by CORE to inform its members and the public about the level of violent opposition to the efforts of the Freedom Summer volunteers. The pamphlet, produced under CORE director James Farmer in the fall of 1964, provides a timeline of violent acts committed against African Americans, civil rights activists, voter registration volunteers, and churches during the summer of 1964. On the front is a grim picture of authorities searching for the bodies of Chaney, Schwerner, and Goodman. The caption reads: "Searching a Mississippi river for bodies of three missing young civil rights workers. Their bodies were later discovered, savagely beaten and bullet-ridden, a black day in the Calendar of Coercion."[48]

The pamphlet offers brief vignettes about acts of violence committed against civil rights workers; on the back is a list of churches "Burned, Bombed Or Otherwise Destroyed In Mississippi June 15 through August 14." The text links the Freedom Summer campaign to CORE's goal of pressuring Congress to pass a voting rights act:

Nowhere is the "passion for the rights of man" more clearly demonstrated in America than in the continuing struggle for civil rights. This is especially true in the deep South where no one takes up this struggle without inviting the more serious consequences. The situation of the Negro citizen in the North is bad enough, but in wide areas of the South, he is subjected to almost unchecked harassment and violence whenever he tries to exercise the rights guaranteed to him by the Constitution, and those who associate themselves with him invite the same penalties.

Through the efforts of COFO, SNCC, CORE, NAACP, and MFDP, the enormity of the opposition to voting rights became apparent to more Americans across the country and the pressure grew on members of Congress to act. Buttons, pinbacks, posters, pamphlets, and flyers proved themselves effective tools that could achieve specific and local policy goals or broader national objectives.[49] These objects also reflected changes occurring within the Civil Rights Movement. Freedom Summer volunteers wore pinbacks marked "Black Power CORE" as they registered voters in the Deep South [FIGURE 4.32]. At that time, the phrase "Black power" meant support for Black political power achieved through the voting process—to which African Americans had been systematically denied access. Electing Black officials who would respond to the concerns of their constituents was at the heart of the strategy of Freedom Summer, and wearing a pinback like this sent a powerful message to those risking their lives to register and exercise the franchise.

SNCC produced a variety of pinbacks in various shapes, sizes, and styles. The small pinback in FIGURE 4.33 features an image commonly used in the material culture of the Civil Rights Movement: the Black and white shaking hands. The illustration draws on imagery used by fraternal organizations of the nineteenth century and was adopted by many civil rights organizations after World War II.

The NAACP pinbacks in FIGURES 4.34–4.39 measure just under 1 inch, each with the message "Member NAACP" and the year of membership; this design remained largely unchanged throughout the twentieth century.

129

The MFDP registered eighty thousand new members during Freedom Summer, and sixteen hundred new voters were added to the polls. The organization elected sixty-eight delegates to attend and be seated at the Democratic National Convention, to take the place of regular delegates who supported segregation. Led by Fannie Lou Hamer, the delegates traveled to Atlantic City, New Jersey, in August 1964, believing that the resistance they suffered would convince the Democratic Party to let them cast their votes for Mississippi. President Lyndon B. Johnson strongly opposed sitting the delegates from the MFDP, and delegations from Texas and Georgia threatened to walk out of the convention.[50]

Hamer's address to the convention's credentials committee, broadcast on live television, brought the concerns of the MFDP to a national audience. President Johnson, fearing that the walkout by Southern states would occur if the MFDP delegates were seated, proposed giving the MFDP two at-large seats for delegates Aaron Henry and Ed King, along with the promise that future delegations would be blocked if they refused to allow Black delegates. The MFDP delegation refused; they felt that given the events in Mississippi over the summer, the Democratic Party should bar the regular delegates and seat all the MFDP's delegation. Hamer famously remarked, "We didn't come all this way for no two seats." The regular delegates, upset over Johnson's proposed two-delegate compromise, walked out of the convention, leaving the seats vacant. Delegates from the MFDP sat in the seats, but Democratic Party staffers removed the seats the next day, preventing anyone from sitting there. The MFDP then left, before President Johnson and vice presidential candidate Hubert Humphrey gave their acceptance speeches. The MFDP delegation was not seated at the Democratic National Convention, but their efforts served to make voting rights a central issue in the 1964 campaign.[51]

Civil Rights leaders understood that they would need to apply further pressure on lawmakers to pass federal legislation

4.34 (TOP LEFT)
NAACP Member pinback, 1", 1960

4.35 (TOP MIDDLE)
NAACP Member pinback, 1", 1961

4.36 (TOP RIGHT)
NAACP Member pinback, 1", 1962

4.37 (BOTTOM LEFT)
NAACP Member pinback, 1", 1963

4.38 (BOTTOM MIDDLE)
NAACP Member pinback, 1", 1964

4.39 (BOTTOM RIGHT)
NAACP Member pinback, 1", 1965

protecting voting rights and outlawing the Jim Crow practices that disenfranchised voters across the South. The executive committee of the Southern Christian Leadership Conference approved the formation of the Summer Community Organization and Political Education (SCOPE) project in December 1964. The goals of the SCOPE project included preparing African Americans for registration and voting, and also for protests if the proposed Voting Rights Act of 1965 was not passed. The SCLC produced a pinback that helped them accomplish those goals [FIGURE 4.40]. The pinback reads: "SCLC SCOPE PROJECT," and its black-and-white design echoes many of the other pinbacks and buttons produced during the 1960s. Like the widely used image of Black and white hands shaking, the combination of black and white invoked the notion that cooperation was necessary between Black and white Americans if the objectives of the Civil Rights Movement were to be accomplished.[52]

The SCOPE project aimed to connect hundreds of mostly Northern volunteers with Black communities across the South to aid in voter registration and community organizing in support of a voting rights act. Chapters were established in Alabama, Florida, Georgia, South Carolina, North Carolina, and Virginia. A flyer produced in April or May of 1965 outlined the project's goals to old and new members and the public:

> **The SCOPE Project of SCLC is an attack on the three basic problems of the South, and in particular, on the problems of the "Southern Negro," disfranchisement, educational deprivation, and poverty. Hopefully it will be a starting point for projects which will continue working on the eradication of these problems in the years ahead.**

The material culture SCLC produced was used to launch an assault on disenfranchisement, and SCLC leaders understood its power to persuade and recruit.[53]

As civil rights organizations such as SCLC pressed for the passage of a voting rights act, they registered citizens to vote in anticipation of its passage, in places where those citizens had been most disenfranchised. The SCLC's SCOPE Project produced a flyer that told organizers how to start their own chapter. The flyer, produced by the Political Education and Voter Registration Department of SCOPE, began with the purpose of the project: "To recruit five hundred (500) or more persons from academic communities of America to work for 10 weeks this summer in 75 blackbelt rural counties and six (6) urban counties" through voter registration drives and political education. The "Procedure" portion of the flyer states that each participating college or university should create a SCOPE unit of faculty and students and elect (or appoint) a chairman, director, program director, secretary, and treasurer. The flyer lists items needed to conduct the project— among them, objects of material culture:

> 3. Materials:
> SCLC will then mail sample of materials and order blanks for materials (leaflets, posters, buttons, applications, etc.) to SCOPE unit. Order blanks for materials should be filled out completely and returned to SCLC immediately.

The "materials" mentioned in the flyer generated funds for SCLC and the SCOPE project, demonstrated support for a voting rights act, helped recruit new members, and informed the public about the impact of voter suppression on African Americans in Southern states.[54] In a May 1965 letter to volunteers, SCOPE outlined its strategy for recruitment and acknowledged the impact of the materials used by volunteers: "In addition to college volunteers, a large number of people reached through various media, including news stories, organizational publications, and word of mouth, as well as general area publicity, applied and were accepted as unaffiliated individuals." "General area publicity" referred to the buttons, pamphlets, posters, and flyers that spread SCOPE's message, recruited new members, and raised funds for the organization's voter registration efforts.[55]

Around fifty-eight SCOPE chapters were established by the summer of 1965; members worked to register voters, address poverty and poor-quality public education, and protect voting rights. Local organizers relied on material culture to achieve their objectives, requesting items from SCOPE. In June 1965, Director Hosea L. Williams wrote to SCOPE workers to assure them that more "material" was headed their way: "Material is in the process of being printed—and will be mailed to you within the week. Therefore, you need not call—requesting such."[56] He subsequently noted to SCOPE

organizers and volunteers in a memorandum with the subject "SCOPE for 1966" that "there are many ways to recruit students. Posters, brochures and buttons are available from SCLC in Atlanta."[57]

In March 1965, SNCC called for a march in Alabama from Selma to Montgomery to support the Voting Rights Act, to condemn the violence and voter suppression in Alabama, and to commemorate the life of SNCC organizer Jimmie Lee Jackson, who had been shot and killed by police while protecting his mother. The Johnson administration feared the march would inhibit the passage of the voting rights bill inching through Congress. Rev. Dr. Martin Luther King Jr. heeded those concerns and did not head to Selma for the march on March 7, 1965. Led by SNCC head John Lewis,

4.40 (LEFT)
SCLC SCOPE project pinback,
.75", 1964–65
4.41 (RIGHT)
SNCC pinback, 1", 1965

marchers were met by local police and Alabama state troopers armed with billy clubs and tear gas on the Edmund Pettus Bridge. On what became known as Bloody Sunday, Lewis and other marchers were badly beaten and the marchers reluctantly retreated. The violence continued throughout that day and night, as deputized members of the Ku Klux Klan attacked and harassed marchers and the residents of Selma. Lewis said, "I thought I saw death" after his skull was cracked by a nightstick. Men on horseback chased marchers back to Brown Chapel, several blocks away, and when they sought sanctuary, the men on horseback followed, attacking and injuring many inside the chapel.[58]

The marchers, joined by King, returned three days later, knelt in prayer, and were again attacked by troopers with billy clubs and tear gas. At King's urging, the marchers retreated from the bridge, but images of the brutal violence had been captured by journalists and generated attention and outrage from Americans across the country. Five days later, on March 15, 1965, President Johnson addressed a joint session of Congress about the necessity of passing voting rights legislation. That same day, a federal judge approved a permit for another march from Selma to Montgomery. Thousands made the fifty-four-mile journey to Alabama's capital during March 21 to 25, compelled by the previous violence and an understanding of the need for legislation protecting voting rights.[59]

Johnson ordered members of the National Guard to protect the marchers during the five-day journey. Marchers in Selma and their supporters across the country wore buttons and pinbacks to show their approval of the marches and the passage of the Voting Rights Act. The pin marked "1965" was produced by SNCC; proceeds from the sale of these objects had helped SNCC to organize the Selma marches and later to continue the broader efforts of the freedom struggle [FIGURE 4.41]. These objects were seen by millions in the United States and internationally when newspapers and magazines featured photographs of marchers wearing and displaying them. Television broadcasts conveyed the purpose of the marches to the public, helping to recruit members and to create a sense of a national movement for civil rights.

After the Selma marches, activists continued to pressure members of Congress to pass the Voting Rights Act. Flyers such as the one in FIGURE 4.42 publicized an SNCC meeting at Albany State University in Albany, Georgia, on April 2, 1965, led by Lafayette Surney. Surney was elected to SNCC's executive committee; he had been Clarksdale project director for Freedom Summer and had participated in the march from Selma to Montgomery. John Lewis was scheduled to speak at the meeting, but he was recovering from injuries sustained on Bloody Sunday. The flyer in FIGURES 4.43 + 4.43A advertised two meetings on the Albany State campus on September 26 and October 31, 1965. These Project Head Start meetings were called to discuss an upcoming speaker series about voter registration efforts in the South in conjunction with the SCOPE Project. Speakers included Bayard Rustin, War on Poverty task force member Edgar May, Lafayette Surney, the SNCC Freedom Singers, and South Carolina voting rights organizer Bill Leue.[60]

As a result of pressure from civil rights organizations, the televised violence in Selma, and the March to Montgomery, the Voting Rights Act of 1965 passed through Congress on August 6. The act's passage was a watershed moment in the Civil Rights Movement and marked the culmination of decades of struggle to outlaw disenfranchisement. The law prohibited states from imposing literacy requirements and poll taxes and sent federal election examiners to polling places to protect African Americans' right to register and vote. Section 2 prohibited the use of skin color or race as a reason to deny or abridge access to voting. Section 5 required "preclearance" to those states covered in the law, meaning that those states had to get approval from the district court of the District of Columbia or the attorney

4.42
**SNCC "Selma" flyer,
8.5 x 11", 1965**

Lafayette Surney, of the national Executive Committee of the Student Non-Violent Coordinating Committee (S.N.C.C.) and a participant in the recent march from Selma to Montgomery is coming to Albany State to speak this Friday. His speech will take place in Page Hall at 1:25 P.M. He is being sponsored by the Freedom Council.

Mr. Surney will speak on his participation in the recent march and on various S.N.C.C. projects in the South, notably the summer registration projects in Mississippi and in Alabama in which he has been active.

He will speak instead of Mr. John Lewis, S.N.C.C. National Chairman, who was originally scheduled for this engagment but was forced to cancel as a result of a fractured skull suffered during a vicious beating at the hands of Alabama state troopers during the dispersion of the first attempt to march from Selma, several weeks ago.

Mr. Surney, a native of Ruleville, Mississippi, has been active in the Civil Rights Movement since 1961, when the Student Non-Violent Coordinating Committee entered Sunflower County, Mississippi to regester Negro voters. He was a project director in Clarksville, Mississippi last summer as a part of last year's Mississippi Summer Project. In February of 1965 he was elected to the Executive Dommittee of National S.N.C.C., the post he now holds.

Mr. Surney is a nephew of George Lee, another Mississippi Negro who was murdered several years ago as a result of his participation in earlier voter regestration drives. Since he was not a white minister it is possible that you have not heard of his death, or have forgotten it. Mr. Surney, himself, in the course of his work in Civil Rights has been arrested more than six times. However, if still free, he will be here this weekend.

LAFAYETTE SURNEY OF S.N.C.C. — FRIDAY, April 2 — 1:25 P.M. — PAGE HALL.

4.43
"Project Head Start" flyer
(front), 8.5 x 11", 1965

THE ALBANY STATE FREEDOM COUNCIL FOR 1965-6

This year marks the second anniversary in the short but active annals of Albany State's Freedom Council. The Council's purpose is to bring news of the Civil Rights struggle here to the campus and to encourage and coordinate all student and faculty activities in that field. To this end the Council has brought several speakers to Albany including Bayard Rustin of the Southern Christian Leadership Council, organizer of the 1963 March on Washington, Edgar May, deputy director of VISTA [the domestic peace corps], Lafayette Surney, assisstent to John Lewis of the Student Non-violent Coordinating Committee [Lewis himself being unable to attend due to the beating he received in the Selma riots last spring], and the SNCC Freedom Singers.

In addition it has sponsored and worked with the SCOPE summer project's unit at State which during the spring semester raised the money to send two Albany students to do voter registra- tion work in the deep south this past summer. Bill Leue, one of the two, will speak at the Council's first open meeting on Septem- ber 26st. The Council has also published a newsletter, held a fruitful program on the American poverty situation at the Golden Eye, helped encourage people to work as tutors in Albany's Arbor Hill and South End slum districts through the downtown Trinity Ins- titute, as well as several other related projects.

This year with the added impetus of a large Student Association budget and with a years experiance under the belt, the outlook for the organization's continued growth and activity is optimistic. There will be numerous speakers, including Senator Jacob Javits of New York, possibly CORE's James Farmer, another ev- ening with the Freedom singers , and several other speakers not yet chosen. There will be continued work with SCOPE, the tutorial project, the newsletter, and numerous other special programs as the current Civil Rights struggle continues all over the country for another year.

All students and faculty members are invited to the first meeting of the Council, as well as any following mmet- ings and events, as either interested observers or members. The first meeting will be this coming Sunday evening, Septem- ber 26, at 7:30 P.M., in Brubacher Hall. As noted above, Bill Leue, a State junior, will speak, and answer questions con- cerning his summer in Allandale County, North Carolina, where he helped register Negro voters with the SCOPE summer project.

4.43A
"Project Head Start" flyer
(reverse), 8.5 x 11", 1965

general before passing any new voting provisions. These measures were enacted to end unconstitutional practices such as violence, voter intimidation, poll taxes, and literacy tests.[61]

The Voting Rights Act and its implementation had a profound impact on increasing voter registration and turnout, particularly among African Americans. African American men had been granted the right to vote in 1870 with the ratification of the Fifteenth Amendment to the Constitution, and women in 1920, after the Nineteenth Amendment, but through systematic disenfranchisement, African Americans were prevented from exercising those rights. For example, only 6.7 percent of voting-age African Americans in Mississippi were registered in 1964. Through the continued voter registration efforts of civil rights organizations such as SNCC, CORE, and NAACP, 59 percent of African Americans were registered by 1967, and by 1969, that number increased to more than 60 percent—above the national average.[62]

As the Civil Rights Movement grew throughout the 1950s and early '60s, so did the use of material culture. Objects such as buttons, pinbacks, posters, and flyers raised awareness among the public about segregation during the sit-in movement. Activists across the country wore CORE buttons to show support for the Freedom Riders, and the sale of those buttons allowed them to support their riders as they were beaten and jailed across the South [FIGURE 4.44]. Objects were used to promote the March on Washington in 1963, and civil rights organizations continued to use them to press for the passage of the Civil Rights Act of 1964. Posters, pamphlets, and pinbacks were key to the efforts of activists combating disenfranchisement. They were used by SNCC volunteers during Freedom Summer and were present at the Selma marches. The sight of peaceful protestors being attacked—many of whom carried signs, held banners, and wore buttons—helped put pressure on members of Congress to pass the Voting Rights Act of 1965.

4.44
CORE "Freedom Now"
pinback, 1.25", 1963–65

Following the passage of the Civil Rights and Voting Rights Acts, organizations, leaders, and activists diverged over the objectives and tactics of the Movement. Some goals had been achieved, but de facto segregation and disenfranchisement remained. Systemic problems such as poverty, poor education, and lack of employment were daily realities for millions of African Americans across the country. Civil rights organizations used the protections afforded in the new legislation to challenge segregation and disenfranchisement through the courts, conduct voter registration drives, and elect candidates, but the hard work of the Civil Rights Movement was not over; it faced stiff, and often violent, opposition.

Visions
of
Freedom
(1966–1980s)

A fter the passage of the Civil Rights Act (1964) and
the Voting Rights Act (1965), material culture helped
civil rights organizations and activists determine
their varied objectives and employ multiple tactics.
Debate continued within the Civil Rights Movement about
goals and methods, but with federal legislation outlawing
racial discrimination and disenfranchisement, two major
victories had been achieved. Despite these protections,
discrimination, disenfranchisement, and violence directed at
African Americans persisted, and many within the Movement
believed its main objective should be to end those injustices,
while others thought it should be to focus on poverty and
employment. There were also different visions for the best
tactics to achieve those objectives. Many saw electoral politics
as the best way to achieve their goals; others believed that
the new legislation was not being widely enforced and that
continued protest and advocacy were still necessary, while
some argued that self-defense was required. All of these

OPPOSITE
**Demonstrators at the
Poor People's March near
the Washington Monument
and Lincoln Memorial,
Washington, DC, June 19, 1968**

145

campaigns used material culture, such as buttons, bumper stickers, pinbacks, and posters, to convey their diverse messages.[1]

At the 1967 National Conference for New Politics (NCNP) in Chicago, Rev. Dr. Martin Luther King Jr. was the keynote speaker because of his strong civil rights platform and opposition to the Vietnam War. The NCNP was a convention of over two hundred organizations, with about a thousand delegates, advocating for civil rights and against the Vietnam War. Groups such as the Lowndes County Freedom Organization and the SCLC discussed supporting reformist presidential candidates like Adam Clayton Powell in New York, Simon Casady in California, and the comedian and civil rights activist Richard C. "Dick" Gregory in Illinois. King was being discussed as a third-party presidential candidate in 1968 and the hope was that he, along with his vice presidential running mate, Dr. Benjamin Spock, could merge the Civil Rights Movement and the peace movement.

The campaign was short-lived because of disagreements within the conference and, possibly, infiltration by the FBI. The pinback in FIGURE 5.1 was produced in 1968 and shows King's portrait against a plain white background. King had become a national spokesman for the Civil Rights Movement, and his image alone could convey a powerful message. FIGURE 5.2 shows a jugate, or double portrait, pinback of King and Spock.[2]

The Peace and Freedom Party (PFP) was founded in 1966, and by 1968, it was a national party running candidates who opposed the Vietnam War. The PFP ran several presidential candidates, and in each campaign, material culture—particularly buttons—helped spread its message. The PFP's first nominee was Black Panther spokesman Eldridge Cleaver. Cleaver won the nomination by a vote of 161 to 54 over Gregory, but he was not eligible to be elected president because he was not yet thirty-five years old. In spite of this, Cleaver campaigned extensively and made it

5.1 (TOP)
"Martin Luther King for President" pinback, 1", 1967
5.2 (BOTTOM)
King/Spock jugate pinback, 1", 1968
5.3 (OPPOSITE)
Lisa Lyons, "Support Eldridge Cleaver for President at the Peace & Freedom Nominating Convention" poster, 17.5 x 23", 1968

onto several ballots in 1968, and his campaign distributed thousands of buttons, posters, and flyers [FIGURE 5.3].[3]

The PFP produced thousands of buttons [FIGURE 5.4] with the dove-and-chains motif. The dove symbolized the party's anti-war stance, and the chains represented the oppression and discrimination it opposed. The buttons were produced in multiple colors that reflected the psychedelic style of the late 1960s. These buttons helped spread the message of the PFP, raised money, recruited members, and helped create a sense that the Civil Rights Movement and the anti-war movement were merging. Eldridge Cleaver's book *Soul on Ice*, published in 1968, helped convey his radical stances on a range of issues, as did the Black Panthers' official newspaper, of which he was the editor; Cleaver understood that wearing and displaying objects with the Peace and Freedom Party's logo, as well as others with his own image, conveyed that message to a wide audience.[4]

Cleaver's nomination created divisions within the party when California courts ruled that he could not appear on the ballots because of his age ineligibility. Dick Gregory was listed as the presidential candidate for the PFP in some states, but when the PFP would not solely back his candidacy, he formed an offshoot party called the Freedom and Peace Party. Gregory led a "write me in" campaign for president, with different vice presidential running mates in various states. FIGURE 5.5 shows a pinback from that campaign urging supporters to write in Gregory "before it's too late." The ease of producing objects like pinbacks allowed candidates like Dick Gregory to adapt their campaigns to changing circumstances and to convey a complex political message.

After King's assassination in April 1968, Gregory was listed on the ballot with King's running mate, Spock, and their visages appear on a jugate pinback in FIGURE 5.6. One of Gregory's other running mates was Dr. David Frost, chairman of New Jersey's branch of the National Committee for a Sane Nuclear Policy; FIGURE 5.7 shows a pinback from his write-in campaign. Gregory's campaign produced thousands of posters,

5.4 (TOP LEFT)
**"Peace and Freedom Party"
button, 1.5", 1968**
5.5 (TOP RIGHT)
**"Before It's Too Late Vote
Gregory in '68" pinback, 1",
1968**
5.6 (BOTTOM RIGHT)
**"Peace and Freedom" Gregory
Spock jugate pinback, 1.25",
1968**
5.7 (BOTTOM LEFT)
**"Dick Gregory for President
David Frost for Vice President"
pinback, 1.5", 1968**

as well as fake dollar bills featuring Gregory's portrait, in
cooperation with Operation Breadbasket. Operation Breadbasket was a department of the Southern Christian Leadership
Conference (SCLC) dedicated to improving poor economic
conditions for African Americans. The Gregory bills caused
some confusion and were reported to work in some vending
machines. The federal government prevented their further
distribution, but the bills helped publicize Gregory's write-in
campaign.[5]

The Voting Rights Act of 1965, and the federal protections it provided, allowed millions of African Americans to
participate in the electoral process—many for the first time.
Enforcement was uneven and slow, but Black candidates began
to run successful campaigns, even in the South. One such

candidate was Charles Evers, who became politically active after he returned from World War II.[6]

Along with his brother, Medgar, Evers joined the Regional Council of Negro Leadership (RCNL) and often spoke about securing voting rights at its annual conference in Mound Bayou, Mississippi. He had become the Mississippi NAACP state voter registration chairman in 1954 but was forced out by white supremacists who threatened his life. Evers moved to Chicago but returned to Mississippi in 1963, after Medgar Evers was murdered by Ku Klux Klan member Byron De La Beckwith. Charles Evers took up his brother's position as field director for the NAACP in Mississippi and began to build a reputation for action.[7]

In 1968, John Bell Williams, the mayor of Fayette, Mississippi, was elected governor of Mississippi, and Charles Evers decided to run for mayor, competing against six white candidates. Evers knew that campaign giveaways—particularly buttons and pinbacks—were vital for publicizing his run and for bringing voters to the polls. The button in FIGURE 5.8 features a portrait of Evers, whose visage was familiar to most Fayette residents. It proclaimed Charles Evers was "The Man Who Cares"—a reference to his years of service to the community. The campaign was successful, and in 1969, he was elected mayor of Fayette—the first Black elected official in Mississippi since Reconstruction—and was named the NAACP's Man of the Year. The button in FIGURE 5.9 was issued in 1969 to commemorate his historic victory. Evers was reelected in 1973, then had unsuccessful runs for the US Senate (in 1978) and for governor (in 1981) but served as an informal advisor on civil rights to several presidents, including Richard Nixon, Jimmy Carter, and Ronald Reagan.[8]

By the late 1960s, the success of the material culture of the Civil Rights Movement in achieving legislative victories impacted the objects produced by other campaigns across the country. Many objects such as the buttons in FIGURES 5.10 + 5.11 were designed to resemble the style of Civil Rights Movement

CHARLES EVERS
"THE MAN WHO CARES"

INAUGURATION
JULY 7, 1969
EVERS
MAYOR
FAYETTE, MISS.

DEMOCRATS FOR EQUALITY

NOW = KENNEDY

VOTE = EQUAL RIGHTS

"These are not ordinary times

KENNEDY KING

I need your hand and your help."

5.13
**Kennedy King handmade bumper sticker, 19.5 x 4.5",
1967–68**

buttons and also reflected the message of the Movement. The Democratic Party and its candidates used imagery and phrasing from the Movement in the buttons and pinbacks they produced, such as the one in FIGURE 5.12, which features the handshake popular in other pinbacks and buttons of the era. Support for civil rights and racial equality became part of the platform of national, state, and local candidates, and material culture was a vital component of that process.

FIGURE 5.13 shows a handmade bumper sticker reading "Kennedy / King," proposing a campaign uniting former attorney general Robert F. Kennedy and Rev. Dr. Martin Luther King Jr. By imagining this ticket and displaying the bumper sticker, the maker was demonstrating support for the Civil Rights Movement and a belief that electoral politics was the best way to achieve the Movement's objectives. It was likely produced in 1967 or early 1968, prior to King's assassination in April and Kennedy's just four months later.

There was an increase in the amount of political material culture produced in the late 1960s and '70s, and none more so than for the Civil Rights Movement. Objects could effect change and also serve as reminders and memorials of the cost paid by those who fought for equal protection under the law and the right to vote. The poster in FIGURE 5.14 was produced by the National Voter Registration Drive and implores the viewer to vote because so many paid the ultimate price, fighting for their right to exercise the franchise.[9]

5.14
"Somebody paid the price for
your right" poster, 16 x 24.5",
1971–72

While electoral politics achieved significant legislative victories and an increase in African American candidates running for office, discrimination, disenfranchisement, and racist violence continued. Many within the Movement believed that continuing the tactics of protest and advocacy was the best way to increase the slow pace of change: sit-ins, boycotts, protests, marches, and demonstrations had proved to be successful methods for combating discrimination and disenfranchisement and had led to the passage of the Civil Rights Act (1964) and the Voting Rights Act (1965).

153

In 1965, Richard C. Boone became a field director for the SCLC in Alabama. Boone had a long history of activism, including helping to organize the marches in Selma. He believed that protest and direct action were necessary tactics to pressure elected officials to enforce civil rights protections. When the SCLC wanted him to transfer to Chicago to continue fighting for voting rights, Boone decided to stay in Montgomery and fight discrimination at home. He worked closely with the Montgomery Improvement Association (MIA), but that group was opposed to his preferred tactic of using protests and demonstrations, so Boone formed the Alabama Action Committee (AAC) in 1967. The AAC organized boycotts of businesses on Montgomery's Dexter Avenue to compel them to hire African Americans, treat Black customers respectfully, and allow Black employees to handle money and supervise whites.[10]

In 1969, the AAC protested discriminatory hiring practices by organizing a second boycott of downtown Montgomery businesses that became known as the "Blackout." The boycott was successful, and material culture such as the button in FIGURE 5.15 helped to spread the word about the AAC, as well as to recruit members and to raise money and support. Following the arrest and beating of Liege Richardson, a Black disc jockey at WPAX, the AAC led demonstrations against police brutality and judicial injustice in Montgomery. The AAC was also concerned about poverty, so they helped distribute food to those in Montgomery who needed assistance. Richard C. Boone became known as the "food stamp man" because he and the AAC were granted approval by the Board of Revenue and the County Commission to bring the federal food stamp program to Alabama, which helped thousands in need. In 2017, Governor Kay Ivey declared July 7 Rev. Dr. Richard Boone Day in the state of Alabama.[11]

The booklet in FIGURE 5.16 was produced in 1967 to promote an October concert series held in San Francisco; Houston; Chicago; Cleveland; Washington, DC; Philadelphia;

5.15 (ABOVE)
Alabama Action Committee button, 1.5", 1969
5.16 (OPPOSITE)
"Stars For Freedom" booklet, 11 x 8.5", 1967

and Boston. Stars for Freedom was an affiliation of singers, musicians, comedians, and actors who used their celebrity status to promote the Civil Rights Movement. The group held concerts and events to raise awareness of civil rights causes and to lift the spirits of those in the Movement, and it created a fundraising infrastructure that aided organizations such as SCLC, SNCC, CORE, and NAACP.[12] The objects it produced helped to publicize the events and also provided information about the work of those affiliated organizations.[13]

The pictured booklet began with a statement from Rev. Dr. Martin Luther King Jr. about the importance of Stars for Freedom. It provided brief biographies of some of the performers, including Harry Belafonte and Joan Baez. It also contained pictures from major events in the Movement such as the Selma marches, as well as a timeline of SCLC's activism, from its founding in 1957 to its tenth anniversary in 1967. One caption for a photo of a demonstration read, "People made the

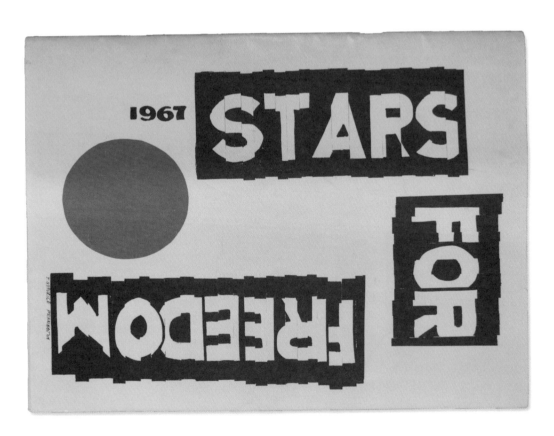

SCLC

332 AUBURN AVENUE, N. E.
ATLANTA, GA.

MEMO: To our Friends
FROM: The SCLC Staff
SUBJECT: SCLC Project Report

May, 1967

SCHOOL INTEGRATION One of the most shameful untold stories in
the South is the day-to-day physical abuse and constant harassment endured by Negro children and their parents in integrating
schools. This year, SCLC is fighting for elementary physical
protection of Negro school children in two particularly vicious
school systems - Wilcox County, Alabama and Grenada, Mississippi,
where white schools were integrated in September. Beatings of
children in and out of the schools took place every day. Some
Negro parents, unable to watch their children being subject to
torment and physical harm, finally pulled them out of the
schools. Recognizing that this could be a disastrous setback
to school integration and conscious of the deep willingness to
take risks, SCLC staff members rallied the Negro community and
168 Negro students returned to the integrated schools. One day,
history will adequately record the heroism of these parents and
children. At this writing, the abuse in both Grenada and
Wilcox has subsided.

SELF-HELP PROJECTS Among the largest and incontestably the
most successful Negro-owned cooperative in the South is the silk
screen plant established in Talieferro, Ga. Established by SCLC
and others to give work to Negroes fired because of their civil
rights activity, it has expanded into garment manufacturing. It
is operating profitably in competitive trade channels and is
already the largest industry in the town.

In Grenada, Miss., work is almost completed on the Negro-owned
and managed cooperative supermarket which grew out of the boycott
campaigns against the discrimination in white stores.

The poverty program which SCLC staff designed and launched in
Wilcox County, Alabama, has been so successful it has burst
over its banks. Planned for 200 families, response has been so
phenomenal the project is running triple sessions at ten
educational centers for over 500 families. (Wilcox County
Negroes, in the midst of America's historic boom, earn $540 per
capita annually.)

SOME IMPORTANT FISCAL FACTS
ABOUT SCLC

- Dr. King receives no salary nor any other
  compensation for his services. A majority
  of our staff, though full-time experienced
  workers, receive only $25 per week. Other
  members of the staff with family responsi-
  bilities average approximately $4,000 per
  year. Their acceptance of these low wages
  reflects their dedication to the movement.

- SCLC is registered with the Charities
  Reg. Dept. of N.Y. State—Reg. #12147.

- Our administrative costs are well below
  the ratio regarded as standard.

- Our books are audited by Jesse B. Blay-
  ton, C.P.A. Our financial statement is
  available to the public.

- Our fund raising is done in the most care-
  ful, economical fashion by our own staff
  and volunteers. We use no commercial
  fund raisers to insure that the largest
  possible portion of your contribution supports active programs.

- Each contributor is kept informed of our
  activities by periodic bulletins.

YOUR CONTRIBUTION TO SCLC SUPPORTS:

- Voter Registration (North & South).
- Action and education programs to end slums.
- Dialogue program for reconciliation of White
  and Negro.
- Citizenship Clinics and Work-shops on nonviolence.
- Direct Action Programs to end segregation
  and self-help economic and political programs.
- Merit Employment Programs to end job discrimination.
- Legal Defense and bail for victims of racial
  injustice.

─── SCLC IS DEDICATED TO ───
helping the American Negro attain
first class citizenship by NON-VIO-
LENT direct action and education.

*"No American can afford to be apathetic
about the problem of racial injustice."*
—*Martin Luther King, Jr.*

SOUTHERN CHRISTIAN LEADERSHIP CONFERENCE
A non-profit, non-sectarian agency
334 Auburn Ave., N. E., Atlanta, Ga.

MARTIN LUTHER KING, JR.   RALPH ABERNATHY
President   Vice Pres.-Treas.

(see other side)

SOME IMPORTANT FISCAL FACTS
ABOUT SCLC

- Dr. King receives no salary nor any other
  compensation for his services. Most of our
  staff receive wages which are either below
  the poverty line or only slightly above it.
  This reflects not their ability or compe-
  tence, but rather their dedication to the
  movement.

- SCLC is registered with various official
  state organizations supervising fund appeals.

- Our administrative costs are well below
  the ratio regarded as standard.

- Our books are audited by Jesse B. Blay-
  ton, C.P.A. Our financial statement is
  available to the public.

- Our fund raising is done in the most care-
  ful, economical fashion by our own staff
  and volunteers. We use no commercial
  fund raisers to insure that the largest
  possible portion of your contribution supports active programs.

- Each contributor is kept informed of our
  activities by periodic bulletins.

─── IF YOU ALREADY ARE ───
A CONTRIBUTOR TO SCLC...
This mailing is being sent to a group
of selected mailing lists other than
our own. It has been proven by care-
ful research that we save money by
not attempting to eliminate duplica-
tion. These mailings, despite their
occasional duplications, enable us to
substantially enlarge the ranks of
our supporters.

YOUR CONTRIBUTION TO SCLC SUPPORTS:

- Voter Registration (North & South).
- Action and education programs to end slums.
- Dialogue program for reconciliation of White
  and Negro.
- Citizenship Clinics and Work-shops on nonviolence.
- Direct Action Programs to end segregation,
  to build self-help economic and political
  projects.
- Merit Employment Programs to end job discrimination.
- Legal Defense and bail for victims of racial
  injustice.

SCLC
A non-profit, non-sectarian agency
334 Auburn Ave., N. E., Atlanta, Ga.

MARTIN LUTHER KING, JR.
President

movement, and people will determine its destiny." Pieces like this booklet were the tools that helped make that possible.[14]

King traced the origins of Stars for Freedom back to the March on Washington for Jobs and Freedom in August 1963. Many celebrities participated in the concerts, including Sammy Davis Jr., Dick Gregory, Sidney Poitier, Ossie Davis, and Ruby Dee. These performers were the core of the Stars for Freedom, but many other celebrities such as Marlon Brando, Lena Horne, Eartha Kitt, Charlton Heston, Paul Newman, and Frank Sinatra risked their careers to promote the Movement.

Stars for Freedom supported the Selma marches in 1965 and organized a show in Montgomery, Alabama, at the end of the second march. After the Selma campaign, Stars for Freedom continued to fundraise for civil rights organizations pressing for the protection of voting rights. SCLC had spent $50,000 organizing the Selma marches, and Sammy Davis Jr. organized a benefit show that raised $150,000. SCLC recouped their losses, and some of the proceeds were given to CORE to send ten volunteers to the Deep South to register voters.[15]

In March 1967, civil rights activists began a third march from Selma to Montgomery to protest the disenfranchisement of African Americans. When the march passed through Lowndes County, Alabama, on March 22 and 23, the county was 81 percent African American but no Black residents were registered to vote. On March 24, thousands of marchers crossed into Montgomery County and assembled in the city of St. Jude. Their spirits were lifted at a Stars for Freedom rally, where singers including Harry Belafonte and Nina Simone performed. The next day, marchers made their way to the state capitol building, where they delivered their petition to Governor George Wallace.[16]

Stars for Freedom was one of the many programs the SCLC was involved in to combat discrimination, disenfranchisement, and violence. Material culture was central to those efforts, and the objects produced allowed SCLC to promote its objectives and raise funds for the

5.17 (OPPOSITE TOP LEFT)
"SCLC Project Report" memo, 5.5 x 8.5", 1967
5.17A (OPPOSITE BOTTOM LEFT)
"SCLC Project Report" memo (reverse), 5.5 x 8.5", 1967
5.18 (OPPOSITE RIGHT)
"Some Important Fiscal Facts about SCLC" insert, 3.5 x 8.5", 1967

157

5.19 (TOP LEFT)
SCLC "I Gave" collection can (front), 2.75 x 6", 1968

5.19A (TOP RIGHT)
SCLC "I Gave" collection can (reverse), 2.75 x 6", 1968

5.20 (BOTTOM)
SCLC "I Gave" card, 3.5 x 2.25", 1968

5.21 (TOP LEFT)
NAACP Member pinback, .75", 1966
5.22 (TOP MIDDLE)
NAACP Member pinback, .75", 1967
5.23 (TOP RIGHT)
NAACP Member pinback, .75", 1968
5.24 (BOTTOM LEFT)
NAACP Member pinback, .75", 1969
5.25 (BOTTOM RIGHT)
"I'm a NAACP Member Join" pinback, 1", 1970

organization. The four-page memo in **FIGURES 5.17 + 5.17A** was sent to thousands of households in 1967 to raise money for the SCLC and to inform the public about their efforts across the country. The memo states, "Your Contribution to SCLC Supports: Voter Registration (North and South), Direct Action Programs to end segregation, and Legal Defense and bail for victims of racial injustice." This memo, dated May 1967, lists those programs and many others, including efforts to integrate schools, Operation Breadbasket, and a "Citizenship Education Program"; an insert [**FIGURE 5.18**] presents "Some Important Fiscal Facts about SCLC."[17]

After King's death in April 1968, the future of SCLC was in doubt. The organization was in need of funding, and the assassination of its leader left many wondering if it could survive. SCLC appointed Rev. Ralph Abernathy as its new president and began a fundraising campaign that used material culture to spread the word. SCLC created objects that featured King's image to encourage donors to support his dream. Collection cans [**FIGURES 5.19 + 5.19A**] were used to raise funds,

159

5.26 (TOP)
NAACP Transportation Committee button with ribbon, 1.5 x 6.5", 1969
5.27 (BOTTOM)
NAACP Over 65 Years "Remember Mississippi" pinback, 2.25", 1974

and the card in FIGURE 5.20 was given to contributors. Both objects featured an image of King delivering a speech next to Abernathy, with the slogan "I gave." The image reminded contributors of King's life and legacy, as well as SCLC's future under his successor.[18]

Civil rights organizations such as the NAACP continued to fight discrimination through lawsuits, public information campaigns, and lobbying. The funds raised from members who wore buttons and pinbacks helped make those efforts possible [FIGURES 5.21-5.25]. Since its founding in 1909, the NAACP had given dated pinbacks to their members following payment of their annual dues—a practice which they continued. The dates encouraged members to continue to donate each year to receive the updated pinback. The NAACP created buttons for specific committees and to mark significant milestones. The Transportation Committee button with ribbon in FIGURE 5.26 was made in 1969 to commemorate sixty years since its founding, and the pinback in FIGURE 5.27 was produced in 1974, ten years after Freedom Summer.[19]

The NAACP grew more than any other civil rights organization during the late 1960s and '70s. Their recruitment and fundraising campaigns were a significant part of that success. The NAACP collection can in FIGURES 5.28 + 5.28A, produced in 1967, encouraged donors to purchase a "Life Membership." Financial stability and increased membership allowed the NAACP to continue their fight against discrimination, disenfranchisement, and violence.[20]

The NAACP filed a case in 1966 on behalf of fourteen Black employees of Duke Power Company in North Carolina, who argued that discriminatory practices prevented Black workers from being hired, promoted, and transferred between departments. The Supreme Court's *Griggs v. Duke Power Co.* (1971) ruling determined that if employers could not demonstrate a business necessity for employment requirements, they had to eliminate requirements that disproportionately disadvantaged African Americans.

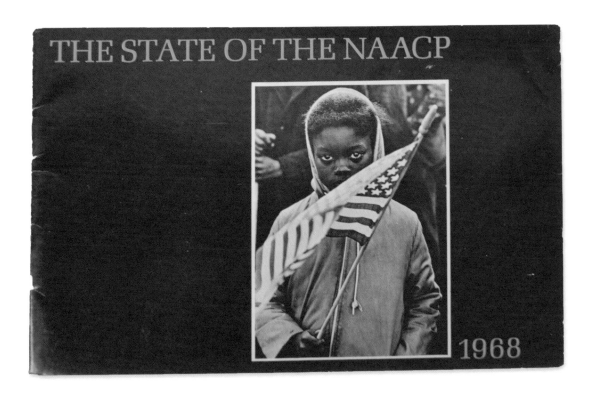

5.28 (BOTTOM LEFT)
**NAACP Honor Guard collection can (front), 3 x 6.5",
1967**
5.28A (BOTTOM RIGHT)
**NAACP Honor Guard collection can (reverse),
3 x 6.5", 1967**
5.29 (TOP)
**"The State of the NAACP"
booklet, 6 x 9", 1968**

The case made a difference in the number of African Americans in the workforce by the second half of the 1970s.[21]

The booklet titled "The State of the NAACP 1968" [FIGURE 5.29] sought to define and defend the organization's tactics of litigation and advocacy. It began with a statement by NAACP Executive Director Roy Wilkins, taken from his speech at the association's annual corporate meeting in New York City on January 13, 1969: "It has been the fashion, now, for the past three years (and particularly since the assassination of Dr. Martin Luther King last April) to predict the death of the civil rights movement." Wilkins goes on to announce that in spite of the "soothsayers'" predictions, and thanks to the diligent efforts of the NAACP, "the civil rights movement is very much alive." The booklet mentions that membership had increased and that they'd raised more than $2.5 million, a $745,000 increase over the previous year. Publications like this booklet helped the NAACP to define its methods in the face of critics: CORE, for example, argued for more direct action rather than litigation and advocacy, claiming that the NAACP "was not relevant."[22]

Opposition to the Vietnam War increased dramatically after 1968, and many aspects of the anti-war movement and the Civil Rights Movement began to overlap. Anti-war organizations used similar tactics to those of the Civil Rights Movement, such as sit-ins and marches, and also used objects like buttons, posters, and flyers to advance their cause. They pointed out that discrimination was rampant in the military and highlighted the inconsistency of fighting for democracy abroad when it did not fully exist at home.

Material culture was used in organize the Moratorium to End the War in Vietnam, a nationwide demonstration held on November 15, 1969, that involved hundreds of thousands of demonstrators across the country. The largest march was in Washington, DC, where nearly five hundred thousand gathered. There were solidarity marches in England and Australia, as well as in Boston, where a hundred thousand

5.30
March on Washington
November 15, 1969
pinback, 1.5", 1969

demonstrated, many of whom wore the pinback in FIGURE 5.30. Flyers sought to link anti-war sentiment with ending discrimination—in particular, police violence—in the United States. On the flyer in FIGURE 5.31, an image of a downtrodden Black soldier sits between the slogans "Self-determination for the Black community" and "End police occupation of the Black community." The flyer in FIGURE 5.32 advertises a march and rally in San Francisco with the phrase "Bring all the troops home now!" The marches were largely peaceful, but President Richard Nixon refused to act on any of the marchers' demands.[23]

African Americans in Wilmington, North Carolina, in the 1960s and '70s, were upset over the persistence of inequality, discrimination, and violence by white supremacists. In January 1971, Rev. Benjamin Chavis Jr. of the United Church of Christ's Commission for Racial Justice went to Wilmington

5.31 (ABOVE LEFT)
"End the War Now!" flyer,
8.5 x 11", 1969
5.32 (ABOVE RIGHT)
"Bring All the Troops
Home-Now!" flyer,
8.5 x 11", 1969

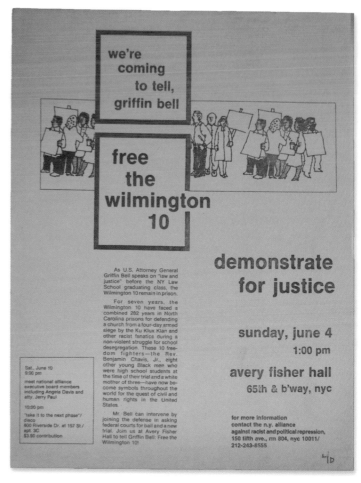

5.33 (LEFT)
"Free the Wilmington 10 Now!" pinback, 1.75", 1971
5.34 (RIGHT)
"Free the Wilmington 10" flyer, 8.5 x 11", 1972
5.35 (OPPOSITE)
Rolando Cordoba, OSPAAAL "Freedom Now!" poster, 18 x 31", 1979

to calm tensions. He preached nonviolence, facilitated classes on African American history, and led boycotts. On February 6, 1971, Mike's Grocery in Wilmington was firebombed, and responding firefighters claimed snipers fired on them from the nearby Gregory Congregational Church, where Chavis and several students were meeting. The National Guard was called to remove the suspects from the building, and the Wilmington Ten, as they became known, were charged with arson and conspiracy and sentenced to a total of 282 years in prison. Activists led a campaign to free the prisoners, producing objects such as the "Free the Wilmington 10 Now!" pinback [FIGURE 5.33] bearing a portrait of Chavis. Thanks to

CLOCKWISE FROM TOP LEFT
5.36
**"We Shall Overcome"
pinback, 1.75", 1970s**
5.37
**"We Shall Overcome"
pinback, 1", 1970s**
5.38
**"United We Shall Overcome"
pinback, 1.75", 1970s**
5.39
**"We Shall Overcome" button,
1.25", late 1960s**
5.40
**"Hope / Hope" button, 1.5",
1970s**
5.41
**Interlocking hands pinback,
1.75", 1970s**

this campaign and materials such as the flyer in FIGURE 5.34 promoting a demonstration in New York City on June 4, 1972, the Wilmington Ten gained international attention.

In 1976, Amnesty International took up the case. Demonstrations continued across the country, including one on June 4, 1978, during US Attorney General Griffin Bell's speech to New York Law School's graduating class. In 1979, the Organization of Solidarity of the People of Africa, Asia, and Latin America (OSPAAAL) produced the poster in FIGURE 5.35 in Cuba as part of a campaign to free the Wilmington Ten. "Freedom for the Wilmington 10" was printed in Spanish, French, English, and Arabic. OSPAAAL was a political movement that grew out of the Tricontinental Conference, which began in 1966 in Havana in order to resist imperialism and globalization and to promote socialism and human rights. The various campaigns garnered international attention and led to exonerations for the Wilmington Ten. In 1980, in *Chavis v. State of North Carolina*, the convictions were overturned, and a pardon was granted to all ten men by North Carolina governor Beverly Perdue on December 31, 2012.[24]

Support for the Civil Rights Movement grew throughout the late 1960s and '70s, as the sentiments, slogans, and imagery of the Movement became part of the fabric of American life. The objects produced, shaped, and reflected the culture, and also helped combat discrimination, disenfranchisement, and violence. Civil rights leaders, activists, and individuals in the 1960s and '70s became adept at using buttons, pinbacks, flashers, flyers, posters, and tabs that featured popularized slogans such as "We shall overcome" and imagery such as Black and white interlocking hands to convey the messages of the Movement [FIGURES 5.36–5.41]. "Keep the faith, baby" [FIGURE 5.42 + 5.42A] was a popular slogan coined by Adam Clayton Powell, who represented Harlem in the US Congress. Other popular phrases, such as those shown on the buttons and pinbacks in FIGURES 5.43–5.46, were worn to show the wearer's support for the Movement.

The notion that African Americans should have political control of their own communities and should defend those communities with force, if necessary, had long roots in the Black freedom struggle. In the late nineteenth and early twentieth centuries, Black lodges and mutual aid societies had provided support to Black communities, and in the 1920s, Marcus Garvey's Universal Negro Improvement Association had over four million members worldwide. In the 1930s, the Nation of Islam (NOI) was founded, and after World War II, the emergence of new nations from colonial rule had a dramatic effect on Black consciousness in the United States through the 1960s. In the face of persistent violence,

5.42 (TOP)
"Keep the Faith, Baby" flasher (position 1), 1.5", 1967
5.42A (BOTTOM)
"Keep the Faith, Baby" flasher (position 2), 1.5", 1967

segregation, and disenfranchisement, some argued that self-defense was a more effective strategy than nonviolent direct action. The failure of the 1964 Civil Rights Act and the 1965 Voting Rights Act to prevent these injustices caused many to support the philosophy of Black control of the Black community.

In 1966, conservatives and white supremacists in New York City began a campaign to eliminate the Civilian Complaint Review Board that provided some community oversight of police activities. Civil rights activists demanded citizen oversight as a way to curb police misconduct and ease tensions between communities and police. African Americans had long complained about police brutality, harassment, and discrimination, but the opposition was able to place the measure on a citywide referendum. Buttons and pinbacks were produced to encourage voters to support the review board [FIGURE 5.47], but New Yorkers voted to eliminate the review panels by a wide margin.

Objects such as buttons, posters, and flyers were used to counter similar efforts and popularize the notion of Black Power. Its most popular symbol, the black panther, has its origins in Lowndes County, a rural county in central Alabama.[25] In 1965, its population was about 80 percent African American. It acquired the nickname "Bloody Lowndes" because white supremacists used violence, intimidation, and voter suppression to prevent any African Americans from registering to vote there. The residents knew that electing Black officials was an effective way to combat the systemic racism, but they needed help to accomplish that task. SNCC had a headquarters in White Hall, a small town in Lowndes County, where they were operating a voter registration campaign. Residents gathered there to discuss how to form a political party and founded the Lowndes County Freedom Organization (LCFO). They planned to run a slate of candidates in county elections, and Alabama law required that every party have a symbol on the ballot.[26]

5.43 (OPPOSITE TOP LEFT)
"A Man Is a Man" button, 2",
late 1960s
5.44 (OPPOSITE BOTTOM LEFT)
"Equal-Rights Now" button,
3.5", late 1960s
5.45 (OPPOSITE MIDDLE)
" = " pinback, .5", late 1960s
5.46 (OPPOSITE TOP RIGHT)
"To Hell with Wallace" button,
3.5", 1972
5.47 (OPPOSITE BOTTOM RIGHT)
"Don't Let Them Destroy the
Civilian Review Board Vote
NO!" pinback, 1.75", 1966

In 1966, LCFO turned to SNCC field secretary Ruth Howard to design a logo. She initially drew a dove, but it was rejected, so she turned to a black panther, the mascot of nearby Clark College. Howard traced the logo, and when she presented it to the LCFO, the reaction was overwhelmingly positive and the LCFO became known as the Black Panther Party (originally the Black Panther Party for Self-Defense). It was seen as a counter symbol to the white rooster used by the Democratic Party, whose slogan was "White supremacy for the right." The LCFO produced a pamphlet with the SNCC slogan "One man one vote." It depicts a black panther versus a white rooster wearing a "NEVER" pinback, which segregationists wore to indicate their opposition to integration (civil rights activists wore the NEVER pins upside down in protest).[27]

SNCC executive secretary James Forman took the drawing to the SNCC office in Atlanta and gave it to Dorothy Miller (now Zellner) to "fix it up." Miller worked with SNCC Communications Director Julian Bond on press releases and articles for the SNCC publication, the *Student Voice*. She altered a few things, making the whiskers more pronounced and filling in the panther's outline to make it all black. Stokely Carmichael (later Kwame Ture) said that members of the LCFO liked the symbol because "it sure can eat up any ol' white fowl." Carmichael asked if he could take the symbol back to California, where it became better known as the emblem for the newly formed Black Panther Party (BPP).[28]

The seeds of the BPP that grew in Oakland, California, had been planted in Alabama, and material culture helped foster that growth. An LCFO handbill formed the basis for the BPP's "10 Point Program"; both programs called for voter registration drives, community nutrition, and local health clinics. The phrase "Black Power" was coined by Lowndes County organizer and former SNCC member Willie Ricks (now Mukasa Dada) in an exchange with Carmichael. Ricks discussed the necessity of an armed struggle to defend the voting rights of African Americans in Alabama. White supremacists enacted punitive measures to deter Black voters, including evicting those who registered from their homes, committing acts of violence against them, and murdering activists. Hundreds of residents who had been evicted formed a "tent city" on Highway 80, which was repeatedly shot at by members of the Ku Klux Klan. SNCC workers went armed to plantations to register African Americans, and when plantation owners and other whites tried to stop them, they were run off. Ricks had praised activist Viola Liuzzo from the steps of the SNCC Freedom House; Liuzzo was then shot and killed by the Klan on March 25, 1965, as she returned from taking an SNCC activist to the Montgomery airport after the Selma to Montgomery marches.[29]

There was never a formal link between the LCFO and the Black Panther Party, but Carmichael helped form a bridge between the two organizations and also acted as a spokesman for the Black Power movement. The black panther symbol was being used widely in the Bay Area by the end of 1966, but the image began to change. Lisa Lyons, a member of the Independent Socialist Club (ISC) at the University of California, Berkeley, recalled that she "chose the Lowndes County Freedom Organization panther for Black Power Day materials, since it was already widely recognized nationally as a symbol of black power by the fall of 1966." It was used at Black Power rallies, Peace and Freedom Party meetings, and "Free Huey [Newton]" rallies, and it was chosen by the leftist organization Students for a Democratic Society (SDS) as their symbol at a conference in Berkeley in 1966. The BPP, along with other organizations, made the black panther a symbol of self-defense of the Black community against discrimination, disenfranchisement, and violence.[30]

The Black Panther Party for Self-Defense was founded in October 1966 by Huey Newton and Bobby Seale, who met when they were both students at Merritt College in Oakland. They were inspired, in part, by the work of the Afro-American

Newton-Cleaver-Seale Defense Fund
P.O. BOX 8641 Emeryville BRANCH
Oakland, Calif.   94608
ENCLOSED IS $_____

NAME_____

ADDRESS_____

CITY_____ STATE_____ ZIP_____

SUBSCRIPTION FORM . . .

THE BLACK PANTHER

BLACK COMMUNITY NEWS SERVICE
PUBLISHED WEEKLY BY THE
BLACK PANTHER PARTY

Enter my subscription for (check box):

	National Subscriptions	Foreign Subscriptions
3 MONTHS (13 ISSUES)	☐ $2.50	☐ $3.00
6 MONTHS (26 ISSUES)	☐ $5.00	☐ $6.00
ONE YEAR (52 ISSUES)	☐ $7.50	☐ $9.00

(please print)

NAME_____

ADDRESS_____

CITY_____

STATE/ZIP #_____ COUNTRY_____
PLEASE MAIL CHECK OR MONEY ORDER TO:

MINISTRY OF INFORMATION
BLACK PANTHER PARTY
BOX 2967, CUSTOM HOUSE
SAN FRANCISCO, CA 94126

SUPPORT YOUR NEWSPAPER —
SUBSCRIBE NOW!

Association—founded at the University of California, Berkeley, by Donald Warden, Donald Hopkins, Otho Green, and Henry Ramsey—and came to believe that African Americans were an oppressed colony in America who could liberate themselves only through the control of their own communities. The BPP formed alliances with many other organizations and were adept at using material culture and the image of the black panther, as seen on the pinback in FIGURE 5.48. The BPP's platform was summarized in their "10 Point Program," adapted from the Lowndes County Freedom Organization, which included self-determination for the Black community, health clinics, full employment, adequate housing, exemption from military service, and an end to police brutality.[31]

The BPP adopted two main programs to defend the Black community and protect their rights. First, they followed the Oakland Police Department when its officers patrolled in predominantly Black neighborhoods. The party's other focus was community services such as after-school programs and medical clinics.

The Panthers were legally armed and wore distinctive black leather jackets, berets, and typically buttons that displayed the black panther logo, the portrait of a leader, or a Black Power slogan. Black Panthers in Oakland wore buttons with a portrait of Huey Newton [FIGURE 5.49].

The BPP promoted its "10 Points" through endeavors that included political campaigns and legal defense funds. The form in FIGURE 5.50 allowed supporters to subscribe to the *Black Panther*, a weekly publication from the party's Ministry of Information in San Francisco. The proceeds were used to support the defense fund of three of the BPP's most influential leaders: its information minister, Eldridge Cleaver, and its founders, Huey Newton and Bobby Seale, who all were imprisoned or on the run between November 1969 and the summer of 1970.[32]

Huey Newton was convicted of manslaughter in September 1968 for the death of an Oakland police officer,

5.48 (OPPOSITE TOP LEFT)
**Black Panther pinback, 1.5",
1966–68**
5.49 (OPPOSITE TOP RIGHT)
**Huey Newton portrait button,
1.75", 1968**
5.50 (OPPOSITE BOTTOM)
**Newton-Cleaver-Seale
Defense Fund subscription
form, 6.75 x 8.5", 1970**

John Frey, and sentenced to two to fifteen years. Frey had pulled over Newton on October 28, 1967, and called for backup. When fellow officer Herbert Heanes arrived, shots were fired, all three men were injured, and Frey died hours later. Newton testified that the officers were facing each other when shots were fired, and no gun was found on Newton. He was given a new trial in May 1970, but the jury was unable to come to a decision. After almost three years of protests and rallies, and a second hung jury, the district attorney failed to file charges again, and Alameda County dropped all the charges.[33]

Two days after the assassination of Rev. Dr. Martin Luther King Jr., Eldridge Cleaver and fourteen other Black Panthers ambushed several Oakland police officers in retaliation for King's assassination. Two officers were wounded, and Panther Bobby Hutton was killed. Cleaver

5.51 (TOP LEFT)
"Free Black Political Prisoners" button, 1.75", 1970
5.52 (RIGHT)
"Lonnie McLucas, a True Revolutionary!" flyer, 4.75 x 4.75", 1970
5.53 (BOTTOM LEFT)
"Free All Political Prisoners" pinback, 1.25", 1968

was charged with three counts of assault but jumped bail and fled to Cuba. He remained on the run for the next seven years, also traveling to France and Algeria before returning to the United States in 1975.[34]

Bobby Seale was arrested for inciting a riot at the 1968 Democratic National Convention in Chicago, but evidence against him was scant. He was sentenced to four years in prison in November 1969 for sixteen counts of contempt of court for outbursts during the trial. In 1970, Seale was put on trial in New Haven, Connecticut, along with eight other Black Panthers, for the murder of fellow panther Alex Rackley. Rackley had confessed, under torture, that he was a government informant, and Seale was charged with ordering his murder. There was a large demonstration in New Haven on May 1, and the jury was unable to reach a verdict. The district attorney dropped the charges, and in 1972, Seale's other convictions were suspended and he was released.[35] The button in FIGURE 5.51 features the black panther behind prison bars with the slogan "Free Black political prisoners." These buttons, and others like them, kept the Black Panthers' cause—and the legal troubles of its leaders—in the public eye.

Lonnie McLucas was one of the "New Haven Nine," along with Bobby Seale. At trial, it was revealed that McLucas and fellow Panther Warren Kimbro had shot and killed Rackley on the orders of national Panther field marshal George W. Sams Jr. McLucas was sentenced to twelve to fifteen years for conspiracy to commit murder. The small flyer in FIGURE 5.52 shows a portrait of McLucas and calls for the courts to "Free The New Haven 9. Free ALL political prisoners." That same sentiment is echoed on the pinback in FIGURE 5.53.[36]

Black Power and a strategy of self-defense began to influence other civil rights organizations that had previously tried to distance themselves from more "militant" groups. Groups that had previously advocated nonviolent direct action such as SNCC and CORE began to work with the Deacons

5.54 (TOP)
SNCC Green, Black, and Red pinback, 1.25", 1968
5.55 (BOTTOM)
CORE "Black Power" pinback, 1.25", 1968

175

for Defense and Justice, an armed group in Mississippi and Louisiana that defended Black communities against attacks from the Ku Klux Klan. According to the Eldridge Cleaver for President Committee, the Black Panther Party "effected a merger with SNCC." The green, black, and red in the pinback in FIGURE 5.54 was worn by members of SNCC as a sign of their African heritage and solidarity with those involved in the freedom struggle across the diaspora. The pinback in FIGURE 5.55 shows CORE's adoption of the Black Power slogan after 1968.[37]

The ascent of Black Power and its associative imagery spread across the country. The flyer in FIGURE 5.56 was distributed at a University of Alabama football game in either 1968 (in reference to the salute given by Tommie Smith and John Carlos at the 1968 Olympic Games in Mexico City) or 1969, the year before the university began recruiting its first African American players. The flyer asks spectators to "LEAVE!" and tells them: "Your presence here at this game makes you an accomplice in this racial terrorism and a co-conspirator in the perpetuation and nourishment of this racist system." This powerful piece of material culture was designed to capture viewers' attention with Black Power imagery and force them to confront the university's racist policy.

This flyer and the activists who wielded it helped to pressure the University of Alabama to recruit African American athletes. Alabama also lost in a crushing defeat to the University of Southern California's integrated team, 42 to 21, to open their season in 1970. The USC Trojans were led by African American players, quarterback Jimmy Jones and running backs Sam Cunningham and Clarence Davis. In 1971, John Mitchell and Wilbur Jackson became the first African American football players at the University of Alabama.[38]

The tactic of self-defense as a response to discrimination, disenfranchisement, and violence continued through the 1970s. Members of the Communist Workers Party (CWP) and

5.56
"Leave!" flyer, 8.5 x 11", 1970

THIS IS A MILITANT DEMONSTRATION. THIS IS A <u>BLACK</u> MILITANT DEMONSTRATION

WE, BLACK STUDENTS AT THIS UNIVERSITY, DRAMATIZE OUR CONTEMPT FOR THE RACIST ATTITUDES OF THE UNIVERSITY OF ALABAMA'S ATHLETIC DEPARTMENT HEADED BY PAUL "BEAR" BRYANT, WHICH PRESCRIBES THAT THERE BE NO BLACK ATHLETES ON THE CRIMSON TIDE FOOTBALL TEAM.
<u>NO BLACK ATHLETES BECAUSE THEY ARE BLACK</u>

    YOUR PRESENCE HERE AT THIS GAME MAKES YOU AN ACCOMPLICE IN THIS RACIAL TERRORISM AND A CO-CONSPIRATOR IN THE PERPETUATION AND NOURISHMENT OF THIS RACIST SYSTEM.

LEAVE!

CLOCKWISE FROM TOP LEFT
5.57
**"Stop the KKK!" button,
2", 1980**
5.58
**STOKES pinback,
1.5", 1967**
5.59
**Nixon-Humphrey-Wallace
November 5 "Strike 3"
pinback, 1.25", 1968**
5.60
**NAACP "18 Vote" pinback,
1.75", 1970**

local African American mill workers joined for a "Death to
the Klan" rally in Greensboro, North Carolina, on November 3,
1979. When members of the Ku Klux Klan and the American
Nazi Party (ANP) arrived to disrupt the rally and opened fire
on the demonstrators, CWP members returned fire. By the
time the gunfight was over, five CWP members were dead
and seven were wounded. In 1980, during the trial of six
Klansmen and Nazis for murder and rioting, it was revealed
that a confidential informant had told the Greensboro Police
Department about the Klansmen and Nazis' plans to use
violence. Federal Bureau of Alcohol, Tobacco, and Firearms
agent Bernard Butkovich—an undercover agent infiltrating
the local branch of the ANP—had provided the guns used in
the murders. The defendants were acquitted on all charges by
an all-white jury, and in 1984, a federal trial ended with the
same result. In a 1985 civil suit, a North Carolina jury found
five members of the Klan and ANP, two Greensboro Police

officers, and their paid informant liable for the wrongful death of one of the CWP members and ordered them to pay $351,000 in damages.[39]

Three members of the CWP, Nelson Johnson, Rand Manzella, and Willena Cannon, were arrested on rioting charges that stemmed from the November 3 rally. The CWP held rallies and sold items to help raise funds for their legal defense and to spread awareness about their case. They produced a "Stop the KKK!" button [FIGURE 5.57] and a flyer for a rally in the Greensboro Coliseum on February 2, 1980, as well as flyers for a rally on May 3, 1980, that called for attending the trial on May 5. The Greensboro district attorney later dropped all rioting charges in November 1980.[40]

Throughout the 1960s, many continued to believe that electoral politics was the best way to achieve the goals of the Civil Rights Movement. The number of Black elected officials slowly rose as African American voters became increasingly influential in local, state, and national elections. Cleveland mayoral candidate Carl Stokes ran on a platform that reflected his working-class upbringing. Stokes was able to use public education, housing, military service, and the law to improve not only his own status but also many others in the community. He was born in 1927; after his father's passing, he was raised in Outhwaite Homes, the nation's first federally funded housing project. He joined the Army in 1945, and after an honorable discharge, he returned to Cleveland to complete his high school diploma, in 1947. He received his bachelor's degree from the University of Minnesota and was admitted to the Ohio State Bar Association in 1957, after graduating from Cleveland-Marshall College of Law. He became a prosecuting attorney for Cuyahoga County until 1962, when he joined the law firm at which his brother, Louis Stokes, practiced. He was elected state representative that year, becoming the first African American elected to the Ohio House. Stokes focused on enforcing civil rights laws, particularly in the workforce, and increasing support for social welfare programs.

Stokes ran for mayor of Cleveland in 1965 but was defeated. He ran again in 1967, and his campaign produced several buttons. The bright orange color of the pinback in FIGURE 5.58 made the support for Stokes clear. Wearing it in public convinced others to support the campaign and demonstrated his broad support in Cleveland. Stokes was elected mayor of Cleveland in 1967 and reelected in 1969. His use of material culture in his campaigns helped him to win and advocate for policies that alleviated poverty and increased employment. During his time in office, he opened up city jobs to African Americans and women. Stokes chose not to run for a third term in 1971.[41]

Democratic presidential nominees began to court African American voters by supporting policies that promoted political and economic equality, and each campaign produced material to spread its message. The "Strike 3" pinback in FIGURE 5.59, however, indicated the dissatisfaction of many voters with the three major presidential candidates in 1968: Republican Richard Nixon, Democrat Hubert Humphrey, and American Independent George Wallace.

Meanwhile, a national campaign for a constitutional amendment lowering the voting age to eighteen began in the late 1960s. The NAACP campaigned for it because it would increase the number of potential voters. The pinback in FIGURE 5.60 was produced for that campaign and helped lead to the passage of the Twenty-Sixth Amendment to the Constitution in March 1971.[42]

The influence of African American voters on national, state, and local electoral politics increased during the 1970s. Ten years after the passage of the Voting Rights Act, potential presidential candidates in 1975 knew that African American voters and whites who supported civil rights could sway the upcoming presidential election. James "Jimmy" Carter made alleviating poverty and supporting civil rights part of his platform and campaigned with Martin Luther King Sr. in 1976. The button in FIGURE 5.61 shows Carter locking hands

5.61 (LEFT)
"Carter for All of US Vote Democratic" button, 3", 1976
5.62 (RIGHT)
Urban League "Vote" pinback, 1.25", 1976
5.63 (MIDDLE)
"A Vote for Yourself Is a No to Wallace" button, 2.5", 1976

with King between the slogans "Carter for all of US" and "Vote Democratic." Because of his support for social and economic programs, Carter was endorsed by the Urban League, which helped bring out voters in cities with the aid of pinbacks like the one in FIGURE 5.62, and with the help of a broad coalition, Carter won the election.[43]

Other campaigns in 1976 used material culture to publicize their candidate and spread their message. The National Black Political Assembly (NBPA) was a meeting of about eight thousand activists, first held in Gary, Indiana, in 1972 to discuss the social and economic crisis facing African Americans. Also known as the Gary Convention, the assembly's goal was to increase the number of Black candidates running for office and to create a Black political party, because the American political system had failed them. At the NBPA convention in 1975, leaders announced the "76 Strategy" of

181

running a presidential candidate in 1976 in order to popularize a progressive agenda in national politics and to pressure the major parties to address poverty and discrimination. The assembly's first choice was Georgia State Representative Julian Bond, but he declined the nomination to pursue a delegate slot to the Democratic National Convention. The NBPA considered Congressmen John Conyers Jr. and Ron Dellums, as well as Dick Gregory, under what became known as the Independent Freedom Party (IFP). The platform of the IFP supported national healthcare, a reduction in defense spending, public ownership of utilities, and progressive tax reform. Each nominee declined, and eventually the candidacy was offered to musician and civil rights activist Frederick Douglass Kirkpatrick.[44]

Kirkpatrick was a cofounder of the Deacons for Defense and Justice, and his candidacy allowed him to represent the IFP and its positions at political forums across the country. He was a singer/songwriter and served as director of folk culture for SCLC. The button in FIGURE 5.63 shows Kirkpatrick sitting with his guitar, with the message "A vote for yourself is a no to Wallace." The slogan encouraged voters to cast their ballot for a third party, something that Julian Bond said African Americans were not prepared to do in 1976, which was a reason he declined the IFP's nomination. The dispute over the nominating process and disagreements over whether its platform should endorse Black nationalism or an integrationist strategy led to the decline of the IFP and the NBPA.[45]

Many within the Civil Rights Movement believed further protest and advocacy were the best tactics to achieve the objective of addressing poverty and unemployment. Material culture allowed demonstrations, festivals, marches, and protests to spread the word that poverty was a civil rights issue beyond each singular event.

A coalition of antipoverty and civil rights groups organized the first Watts Summer Festival in 1966 as a way to annually celebrate Black heritage and culture on the

anniversary of the Watts Rebellion (or so-called Watts Riots),
sparked by the violent arrest of Marquette Frye, a twenty-
one-year-old African American motorist, for drunk driving on
August 11, 1965. His brother, Ronald, tried to stop the arrest
because he believed the officers were using excessive force.
Frye's mother, Rena Price, was arrested for trying to intervene,
and when more officers arrived, they assumed the onlookers
were hostile and a scuffle broke out between an officer and
someone in the crowd. The resulting six days of rioting were,
in part, due to the arrest, but the larger cause of the unrest
was frustration over decades of racial segregation, police
brutality, and poverty. The diverse coalition's shared goal was
community empowerment and self-definition. At the festivals,
attendees could visit booths run by the Afro-American
Association, the Sons of Watts Improvement Association,
and antipoverty agencies such as the Westminster Neighborhood Association and the Watts Labor Community Action

Committee (WLCAC). The grand marshal for the 1966 festival was Sargent Shriver, the director of the federal initiative the War on Poverty, and in 1967, the organizers chose Muhammad Ali for that role. The material culture produced, which included the button in FIGURE 5.64, was sold to finance the festival but also, afterward, to promote the goal of economic self-empowerment in the Black community.[46]

At a staff retreat in May 1967, SCLC President Rev. Dr. Martin Luther King Jr. declared that the Civil Rights Movement had entered a "new era," a revolutionary phase that sought to address the economic consequences of generations of Jim Crow. Like many others, he became focused on alleviating poverty and increasing employment, as well as on ending the Vietnam War, which disproportionately impacted the poor and African Americans. The SCLC had previously addressed economic insecurity when it established Operation Breadbasket, which aimed to increase Black employment, in 1962. King and Ralph Abernathy believed that something dramatic, "a new and unsettling force," was necessary to galvanize support for this economic message. Civil rights protections were important, but millions were suffering in poverty and wanted opportunity. King announced the Poor People's Campaign, which called for a march in Washington, DC, in 1968. Among the objectives was to lobby Congress for an "economic bill of rights" and to oppose the Vietnam War. Material culture was a vital part of this effort. The sale of pinbacks and buttons [FIGURES 5.65 + 5.66] helped finance and publicize the march, and afterward reminded others about the purpose of the campaign.[47]

King arrived in Memphis on March 18, 1968, to help the sanitation workers' union gain recognition from the city and to campaign for the end of abusive and discriminatory practices against African American employees, including low pay, dangerous conditions, unpaid overtime, and arbitrary termination. This was part of King's belief that economic equality was necessary if African Americans were to exercise

5.65 (OPPOSITE TOP LEFT)
"Poor People's Campaign for Poor Power" button, 3.5", 1968
5.66 (OPPOSITE TOP RIGHT)
"Poor People's Campaign" button, 2", 1968
5.67 (OPPOSITE BOTTOM RIGHT)
P.C.L.C – S.C.L.C. "I Have a Dream" button, 3.5", 1968
5.68 (OPPOSITE BOTTOM LEFT)
"Poor People's Campaign Puertorriqueños Marchan" pinback, 2", 1968

185

their constitutional rights. Material culture was produced for the planned march, and striking workers held protest signs reading "I AM A MAN."[48]

King was assassinated at the Lorraine Motel in downtown Memphis on April 4, 1968, by James Earl Ray, a segregationist and volunteer in the George Wallace presidential campaign. Cities across the United States erupted in riots over the pain and frustration of his murder by an avowed white supremacist. Rev. Ralph Abernathy became president of the SCLC, but King's death marked the end of an era for the Civil Rights Movement. It was a blow to the nonviolent direct-action strategy he had championed, and many questioned its validity altogether. Abernathy and the SCLC decided that the June march on Washington must go on and used material culture to inform the public. The button in FIGURE 5.67 pairs King with Abernathy, along with the familiar "I have a dream" quote from King's speech at the 1963 March on Washington for Jobs and Freedom.[49]

The Poor People's Campaign continued to plan a march through Washington, DC, to show their commitment to King's use of nonviolent protest and to advocate for an end to the Vietnam War and an "economic bill of rights." This "Second Bill of Rights" had been proposed by President Franklin D. Roosevelt during his State of the Union address on January 11, 1944. Roosevelt had argued that political rights alone were not enough to achieve "equality in the pursuit of happiness" and that Americans needed an economic bill of rights to achieve that goal. He proposed the right to employment, food, clothing, shelter, leisure, fair income, housing, medical care, education, and freedom from monopolies. In that spirit, on May 12, 1968, Coretta Scott King, Rev. Dr. Martin Luther King's widow, began a two-week protest in Washington, DC, over the cutting of funding for the early childhood education program Head Start and the stigmatization of those receiving welfare, particularly African American women. On May 13, the first of nine main caravans of self-identified poor people

5.69 (ABOVE)
**Rev. Martin Luther King Jr.
memorial fan, 7.5 x 12", 1971**

5.70 (RIGHT)
**"The Dream Lives On" button,
2.25", 1986**

made its way to the nation's capital. The first had departed from Marks, Mississippi, and other caravans had originated in Los Angeles, San Francisco, Seattle, and the Edmund Pettus Bridge in Selma, Alabama.[50]

Construction began on May 21, 1968, on the National Mall, of a shanty town to house the growing number of marchers; it was named "Resurrection City." A "Solidarity Day" was initially scheduled for May 30 but was postponed by Ralph Abernathy until June 8. Bayard Rustin had been appointed to organize the demonstration but was removed due to his insistence that the economic bill of rights be the sole focus; Abernathy disagreed and thought the goals should include opposition to the Vietnam War.[51]

The residents, along with the rest of the nation, were stunned after hearing the news of Robert F. Kennedy's assassination on June 5, 1968. The grief and confusion did not help with disagreements among the Poor People's Campaign organizers over the purpose and future of the demonstration. Many insisted that ending the Vietnam War become a formal demand, and marches and workshops were held to raise that concern among the public and the participants. Along with African Americans, other people of color such as Native Americans and Puerto Ricans were also disproportionately sent to Vietnam. A "Puertorriqueños Marchan" was organized for June 8; the pinback in FIGURE 5.68 was produced to promote it.[52]

On June 20, police fired tear gas canisters into Resurrection City, but the residents remained. The permit from the city expired on June 23, and on June 24, police arrived to remove the remaining demonstrators. Many remained, singing and clapping, and police arrested 288 protestors, including Abernathy. That afternoon, the mayor of Washington, DC, declared a state of emergency, and riot police began patrolling the streets.

Following the demonstrations, an economic bill of rights was not passed and the United States escalated the war in Vietnam, but some progress was made, including restored funding for Head Start in Mississippi and Alabama. The SCLC organized a "mule train" to lead a march past the Republican National Convention in Miami in early August, and at the Democratic National Convention in Chicago later that month. After Richard Nixon's victory, he met with a Poor People's Campaign delegation and discussed ways to address hunger and malnutrition. The Poor People's Campaign created "Resurrection City II" in Miami at the Democratic National Convention in 1972.[53]

Material culture was used to honor and memorialize King's life and legacy. Churches and funeral homes across the country used fans with his portrait [FIGURE 5.69]. In 1971, several cities, including St. Louis, Missouri, created holidays honoring King, and a campaign began to establish a federal holiday. The button in FIGURE 5.70 was produced to propose January 15, his birthday, as the date. President Ronald Reagan signed a bill on November 2, 1983, and the Birthday of Rev. Dr. Martin Luther King Jr. was first observed as a federal holiday on January 20, 1986. In 1992, President George H. W. Bush declared that the holiday would be celebrated on the third Monday of January, although it was not celebrated by all fifty states until 2000.[54]

Many organizations continued to promote the idea that poverty was the most pressing civil rights issue and that rather than reliance on elected officials or protests, economic self-defense was the best way to achieve equality. Material culture was produced to inform the public of the organizations' platforms, recruit members, raise money, and promote their programs. The booklet in FIGURE 5.71, *Where It's At: A Research Guide for Community Organizing*, was produced by the Radical Education Project (REP) in 1967. REP was founded in 1966 in Ann Arbor, Michigan, by a group of Students for a Democratic Society (SDS) volunteers. It was a nonprofit research and publishing organization designed to promote a "New Left" in America. REP sponsors included Julian Bond

5.71 (OPPOSITE)
**"Where It's At" booklet,
8.5 x 10.75", 1967**
5.72 (ABOVE)
**Black Economic Union "Food
First" button, 2.5", 1970**

and the historian Howard Zinn. Some of the organizations that distributed *Where It's At* were SDS, SNCC, and the Southern Student Organizing Committee (SSOC). It offers ways to organize communities for economic self-reliance and to navigate agencies that could provide assistance. It includes sections about urban renewal, public housing, community services, unions, and jobs. The imagery on the cover and throughout the booklet links the REP's economic message to the broader Civil Rights Movement. The cover features recognizable buttons from several civil rights organizations, including SNCC, CORE, SSOC, and the Mississippi Freedom Democratic Party (MFDP), acknowledging the material culture of the Movement as an effective way to promote its objectives.[55]

The belief that basic needs must be met before political rights can be exercised was a notion championed by the Black Economic Union (BEU; first called the Negro Industrial and Economic Union) and reflected in its program Food First. The BEU was started by the professional football player Jim Brown

191

in 1968 to help African Americans compete in business. In 1970, the BEU funded the Food First program in Holly Springs, Mississippi. Brown had heard that the community was destitute and wanted to provide immediate assistance. Ohio representative Louis Stokes commended Brown, stating, "It was not a very fancy program, or a fancy goal— get food to starving people and get it there fast." To help raise money for the BEU and Food First, the tennis professional Arthur Ashe played a benefit match, and to promote the program, the BEU produced the orange buttons in FIGURE 5.72. Programs such as Food First helped thousands suffering in poverty, but the need was growing.[56]

The Black Panther Party for Self-Defense also believed in alleviating poverty, and much of its "10 Point Program" was about economic improvement through self-determination, particularly in employment and housing. The program includes the statement "We believe that black people will not be free until we are able to determine our own destiny." Jobs, decent housing, and education were necessary for African

5.73 (LEFT)
"Soul Brother" patch, 2.5", 1970s
5.74 (RIGHT)
"Right On" patch, 2.75", 1970s

Americans to achieve political equality and exercise their
constitutional rights. In the 1970s, Black Panthers, and those
who identified with their beliefs, wore patches to indicate their
support for the BPP's platform in FIGURES 5.73 + 5.74. The BPP
wanted to directly help those who were suffering the economic
effects of generations of Jim Crow, favoring immediate action
over more indirect tactics such as electing candidates or
planning symbolic events.[57]

After 1965, those in the Civil Rights Movement differed
over objectives and tactics. Many believed that using the
Civil Rights Act and the Voting Rights Act to combat discrimination, disenfranchisement, and violence should remain
the Movement's focus, while others thought that since some
legislative victories were achieved, alleviating poverty should
become the main focus. Organizations and activists often
worked together on shared goals but continued to disagree
over the best tactics to achieve them. For some, the Civil Rights
Movement ended after the 1960s or '70s, but many of the same
problems persisted through the twentieth century and into
the present day. The Movement's objectives and tactics
continue to evolve, but material culture will always play a
significant role.

AFTERWORD

The events of the past generation have continuously demonstrated that the Civil Rights Movement is not over. The struggle for equal rights in the United States of America is not a linear process with a final result. This has proved to be true throughout the Movement and will continue as long as Americans hold racist beliefs and the effects of structural racism are still being felt.

The sad fact is that too many people believe that Black Americans are not equal citizens of the United States—or even equally human. The impact of that belief is both personal and systemic, and the evidence is all around us. Black Americans face generational poverty, underfunded schools, housing and employment discrimination, voter suppression, and police violence because many Americans want it that way. Everyone has witnessed someone using racial epithets, and since 2016 many have felt more comfortable expressing their racist beliefs in public.

195

Former President Donald Trump brought racist language and policies into the White House, which was met by his supporters with glee rather than condemnation. This is not because he presented new ideas but rather because he was willing to openly express the white supremacist ideology long used by reactionaries who opposed the gains of the Movement.

Once again, Black activists and their allies have had to mobilize against white Americans who want a return to the segregated past. Elected officials have found ways to minimize the Black vote through racially gerrymandered districts and limited access to polling places and the vote. They want African Americans to remain a permanent under-resourced labor class, or worse, and Black activists, citizens, and elected officials across the nation are laboring to preserve the hard-won gains of the twentieth century's movement for justice and equity.

The Black Lives Matter movement protests held across the country, beginning in 2013, became national flashpoints after the murder of George Floyd in 2020. The protests during that summer were one of the largest sustained mass movements in American history—rooted in the fact that for the majority of our nation's existence, the self-evident statement "Black lives matter" has not been the case. More than a decade of video evidence has proved beyond contest that police officers harass, assault, and kill Black Americans. It is institutional racism that affords these officers a lack of charges (or dropped charges), supports laws that make their conviction unlikely, and allows for communities of color to continue to be brutalized.

Black Lives Matter activists are attempting to use many of the tried-and-true tactics of the Civil Rights Movement, including the use of material culture. As the world watched, Black Lives Matter demonstrations and protests were broadcast on television, published in newspapers, and shared across social media. Clearly visible in all of them were signs, buttons, T-shirts, banners, and masks with slogans like "Black lives matter," "My skin color does not determine my worth," "My dad is not a threat," "Silence is violence," and "Racism is a pandemic, too," as well as portraits of George Floyd, Breonna Taylor, Ahmaud Arbery, and others killed by police. This shows that even in a digital age, material culture remains vital to the success of the Movement, and my hope is that *Making the Movement* will serve as a guide for current, and future, activists.

ACKNOWLEDGMENTS

There are so many people who have helped make *Making the Movement* possible, and I could never thank them enough.

Thanks to my parents, David M. Crane and Judith P. Crane, for a lifetime of love and support.

All my love to my beautiful wife, Jennifer. Thank you for your understanding while I worked on "the book."

Thanks to the late Dr. Julian Bond. He began as a civil rights icon, but became a friend.

Thanks to the late Congressman John Lewis for getting in "good trouble."

Making the Movement would like to acknowledge the many organizations that produced the artifacts in this book, and want to thank them for the contributions they made to the fight for freedom, justice, and equality:

National Association for the Advancement of Colored People; Knights of Pythias of North America, South America, Europe, Asia, Africa, and Australia; Owl's Club; National Negro Business League; Universal Negro Improvement Association; International Labor Defense; Congress of Racial Equality; Fellowship of Reconciliation; Southern Christian Leadership Conference; Student Nonviolent Coordinating Committee; Committee to Defend Martin Luther King Jr.; Brotherhood of Sleeping Car Porters; Regional Council of Negro Leadership; Southern Student Organizing Committee; United Freedom Movement; Urban League; Leadership Conference on Civil Rights; Harlem Parent's Committee; Parent's Workshop for Equality; Allied Organization for Civil Rights; Coordinating Council of Community Organizations; Council of Federated Organizations; Mississippi Freedom Democratic Party;

National Conference for New Politics; Peace and Freedom
Party; National Voter Registration Drive; Alabama Action
Committee; Stars for Freedom; Moratorium to End the
War in Vietnam; Organization of Solidarity of the People of
Africa, Asia, and Latin America; Lowndes County Freedom
Organization; Black Panther Party; Deacons for Defense
and Justice; Communist Workers Party; National Black
Political Assembly; Independent Freedom Party; Watts Labor
Community Action Committee; Poor People's Campaign;
Radical Education Project; Students for a Democratic Society;
Black Economic Union; Black Lives Matter.

Special thanks to other institutions and individuals for
their support of *Making the Movement*:

The Robert H. Jackson Center, Syracuse University,
Community Folk Art Center, Allegheny College, Elon
University, the American Political Items Collectors, Busy
Beaver Button Co., William Davis, Ted Hake, and Silas Munro.

Participants in the
civil rights march from
Selma to Montgomery
in March 1965

NOTES

Silas Munro: Bearing Witness
——

Epigraph: James Baldwin, "The Artist's Struggle for Integrity," 1962 WBAI Broadcast, Pacifica Radio Archives, accessed February 25, 2022, https://www.pacificaradioarchives.org/recording/bb3641.

1. Jonathan Senchyne, "Bottles of Ink and Reams of Paper: *Clotel*, Racialization, and the Material Culture of Print," in *Early African American Print Culture*, ed. Lara Langer Cohen and Jordan Alexander Stein (Philadelphia: University of Pennsylvania Press, 2012).

2. Amber Esseiva, *Great Force* (Richmond, VA: Institute for Contemporary Art at Virginia Commonwealth University, 2019), exhibition catalog.

3. Whitney Battle-Baptiste and Britt Rusert, eds., *W. E. B. Du Bois's Data Portraits: Visualizing Black America* (New York: Princeton Architectural Press, 2018).

4. "History of *The Crisis*," NAACP, accessed February 11, 2022, https://naacp.org/find-resources/history-explained/history-crisis.

5. Tasheka Arceneaux-Sutton, "A Black Revolutionary Woman: Louise E. Jefferson," in *Baseline Shift: Untold Stories of Women in Graphic Design History*, ed. Briar Levit (New York: Princeton Architectural Press, 2021).

6. "Am I not a man and a brother?" Library of Congress Prints and Photographs Online Catalog, accessed December 20, 2021, https://www.loc.gov/pictures/item/2008661312/.

7. Ashley Southall and Jonah E. Bromwich, "2 Men Convicted of Killing Malcolm X Will Be Exonerated After Decades," *New York Times*, November 17, 2021, https://www.nytimes.com/2021/11/17/nyregion/malcolm-x-killing-exonerated.html.

8. Billy X Jennings, "Remembering the Black Panther Party Newspaper, April 25, 1967–September 1980," *San Francisco Bayview*, May 4, 2015, https://sfbayview.com/2015/05/remembering-the-black-panther-party-newspaper-april-25-1967-september-1980/.

9. Stephen Coles, "This Just In: Emory Douglas & *The Black Panther*," Letterform Archive, accessed February 15, 2022, https://letterformarchive.org/news/view/emory-douglas-and-the-black-panther.

10. Virgie Hoban, "'Discredit, disrupt, and destroy': FBI records acquired by the Library reveal violent surveillance of Black leaders, civil rights organizations," *Berkeley Library News*, January 18, 2021, https://news.lib.berkeley.edu/fbi.

11. Coles, "This Just In."

Chapter One
——

1. Charles H. Brooks, *The Official History and Manual of the Grand United Order of Odd Fellows in America* (Philadelphia: Odd Fellows' Journal Print, 1902); Michael Barga, "Grand United Order of Odd Fellows in America (1843–present)," VCU Libraries Social Welfare History Project, Virginia Commonwealth University, October 2, 2017.

2. Brooks, *Official History*, 7–15.

3. Marilyn T. Peebles, *The Alabama Knights of Pythias of North America, South America, Europe, Asia, Africa, and Australia: A Brief History* (Lanham, MD: University Press of America, 2012); Hugh Goold Webb, *A History of the Knights of Pythias and Its Branches and Auxiliary; Together with an Account of the Origin of Secret Societies, the Rise and Fall of Chivalry and Historical Chapters on the Pythias Ritual* (1910; repr., London: Forgotten Books, 2015).

4. Peebles, *Alabama Knights*.

5. Peebles, *Alabama Knights*, 12.

6. "Born in the Wake of Freedom," Library of Virginia, accessed December 17, 2017, http://www.lva.virginia.gov/exhibits/mitchell/index.htm.

7. Robert Behre, "100 Years Later, Charleston Black Fraternal Society Still 'About Nothing,'" *Post and Courier*, November 29, 2014, https://www.postandcourier.com/archives/years-later-charleston-black-fraternal-society-still-about-nothing/article52938e7b-00eb-56d3-9355-d7905d566744.html.

8. Michael Rudolph West, *The Education of Booker T. Washington: American Democracy and the Idea of Race Relations* (New York: Columbia University Press, 2008).

9. West, *Education of Booker T. Washington*; Joy James, *Transcending the Talented Tenth: Black Leaders and American Intellectuals* (New York: Routledge, 1997).

10. Mark Stafford, *W. E. B. Du Bois: Scholar and Activist* (Philadelphia: Chelsea House, 2005); David Levering Lewis, *W. E. B. Du Bois: The Fight for Equality and the American Century, 1919–1963* (New York: Henry Holt, 2001); West, *Education of Booker T. Washington*.

11. Joseph Bernardo, "National Negro Business League (1900–)," BlackPast, November 26, 2008, https://www.blackpast.org/?s=national+negro+business+league; Richard Wormser, "National Negro Business League," The Rise and Fall of Jim Crow: Jim Crow Stories, WNET, https://www.thirteen.org/wnet/jimcrow/stories_org_business.html, 2002.

12. Paul Harvey, "Richard Henry Boyd: Black Business and Religion in the Jim Crow South," in *Portraits of African American Life since 1865*, ed. Nina Mjagkij (Lanham, MD: Rowman & Littlefield, 2003), 51–67.

13. Paul Harvey, "'The Holy Spirit Come to Us and Forbid the Negro Taking a Second Place': Richard H. Boyd and Black Religious Activism in Nashville," in *Tennessee History: The Land, the People, and the Culture*, ed. Carroll Van West (Knoxville: University of Tennessee Press, 1998), 270–86; Bobby L. Lovett, *A Black Man's Dream: The First One Hundred Years; The Story of R. H. Boyd* (Nashville: Mega Corporation, 1996).

14. Patricia Sullivan, *Lift Every Voice: The NAACP and the Making of the Civil Rights Movement* (New York: New Press, 2010); Kevern Verney and Lee Sartain, eds., *Long Is the Way and Hard: One Hundred Years of the NAACP* (Fayetteville: University of Arkansas Press, 2009).

15. Stafford, *W. E. B. Du Bois*; West, *Education of Booker T. Washington*.

16. Eugene F. Provenzo Jr., *W. E. B. Du Bois's Exhibit of American Negroes: African Americans at the Beginning of the Twentieth Century* (Lanham, MD: Rowman & Littlefield, 2013).

17. Provenzo, *W. E. B. Du Bois's Exhibit*.

18. Jack Greenberg, *Crusaders in the Courts: Legal Battles of the Civil Rights Movement* (New York: Twelve Tables, 2004); Sullivan, *Lift Every Voice*.

19. Sullivan, *Lift Every Voice*.

20. NAACP, *Thirty Years of Lynching in the United States, 1889–1918* (1919; repr., Clark, NJ: Lawbook Exchange, 2012).

21. Sullivan, *Lift Every Voice*.

22. NAACP, "The Moorfield Storey Membership Drive for 50,000 Members," *Crisis*, March 1918, 219–20.

23. NAACP, "National Association for the Advancement of Colored People," *Crisis*, May 1918, 2.

24. Daniel W. Aldridge III, *Becoming American: The African American Quest for Civil Rights, 1861–1976* (Wheeling, IL: Harlan Davidson, 2011).

25. Woodrow Wilson, *War Messages*, 65th Cong., 1st Sess. Senate Doc. No. 5, Serial No. 7264, Washington, DC, 1917, accessed December 30, 2017, World War I Document Archive, https://wwi.lib.byu.edu/index.php/Wilson%27s_War_Message_to_Congress.

26. Adam P. Wilson, *African American Army Officers of World War I: A Vanguard of Equality in War and Beyond* (Jefferson, NC: McFarland, 2015), 39.

27. Aldridge, *Becoming American*; Sullivan, *Lift Every Voice*.

28. Arthur E. Barbeau and Florette Henri, *The Unknown Soldiers: Black American Troops in World War I* (Philadelphia: Temple University Press, 1974).

29. Walter Dean Myers and Bill Miles, *The Harlem Hellfighters: When Pride Met Courage* (New York: HarperCollins, 2006); Peter N. Nelson, *A More Unbending Battle: The Harlem Hellfighters' Struggle for Freedom in WWI and Equality at Home* (New York: Basic Civitas, 2009); Jeffrey T. Sammons and John H. Morrow Jr., *Harlem's Rattlers and the Great War: The Undaunted 369th Regiment and the African American Quest for Equality* (Lawrence: University Press of Kansas, 2014).

30. Sammons and Morrow, *Harlem's Rattlers*.

31. Cameron McWhirter, *Red Summer: The Summer of 1919 and the Awakening of Black America* (New York: Henry Holt, 2011).

32. W. E. B. Du Bois, "Opinion: Returning Soldiers," *The Crisis*, May 1919, 13–14.

33. Sullivan, *Lift Every Voice*.

34. Mary J. Rolinson, *Grassroots Garveyism: The Universal Negro Improvement Association in the Rural South, 1920–1927* (Chapel Hill: University of North Carolina Press, 2008); E. David Cronon, *Black Moses: The Story of Marcus Garvey and the Universal Negro Improvement Association* (1955; repr., Madison: University of Wisconsin Press,

2001); Wilson Jeremiah Moses, *The Golden Age of Black Nationalism, 1850–1925* (1978; repr., New York: Oxford University Press, 2009).

35. Moses, *Golden Age of Black Nationalism*; Aldridge, *Becoming American*.

36. Henry Louis Gates Jr. and Jennifer Burton, eds., *Call and Response: Key Debates in African American Studies* (2008; repr., New York: W. W. Norton, 2011).

37. Marcus Garvey, *The Marcus Garvey and Universal Negro Improvement Association Papers: The Caribbean Diaspora, 1921–1922*, vol. XIII, ed. Robert A. Hill, John Dixon, Mariela Haro Rodriguez, and Anthony Yuen (Durham, NC: Duke University Press, 2016), 255.

38. Moses, *Golden Age of Black Nationalism*; Aldridge, *Becoming American*.

39. Ramla Bandele, "Understanding African Diaspora Political Activism: The Rise and Fall of the Black Star Line," *Journal of Black Studies* 40, no. 4 (2010): 745–61.

40. William B. Hixson Jr., "Moorfield Storey and the Defense of the Dyer Anti Lynching Bill," *New England Quarterly* 42, no. 1 (March 1969), 65–81; Christopher Waldrep, *African Americans Confront Lynching: Strategies of Resistance from the Civil War to the Civil Rights Era* (Lanham, MD: Rowman & Littlefield, 2008).

41. Sullivan, *Lift Every Voice*.

42. Platform adopted by the National Negro Committee, printed document, 1909. NAACP Records, Manuscript Division, Library of Congress, Washington, DC (019.00.00).

43. Jon E. Taylor, *Freedom to Serve: Truman, Civil Rights, and Executive Order 9981* (London: Routledge, 2013); Kermit L. Hall and Kevin T. McGuire, eds., *The Judicial Branch* (New York: Oxford University Press, 2005).

44. Shana Alexssandra Russell, "Domestic Workers, Sex Workers, and the Movement: Reimagining Black Working-Class Resistance in the Work of William Attaway, Richard Wright, and Alice Childress, 1935–1960" (PhD diss., Rutgers University, 2015).

45. Richard C. Cortner, *A "Scottsboro" Case in Mississippi: The Supreme Court and Brown v. Mississippi* (Jackson: University Press of Mississippi, 2012).

46. "Haywood Patterson Turns to Us," *Labor Defender*, May 1933, 21.

47. Sullivan, *Lift Every Voice*.

48. NAACP, "New Crusade for Liberty Launched," *Crisis*, February 1938, 55.

Chapter Two

1. Neil A. Wynn, *The African American Experience during World War II* (Lanham, MD: Rowman & Littlefield, 2011).

2. Cornelius L. Bynum, *A. Philip Randolph and the Struggle for Civil Rights* (Urbana: University of Illinois Press, 2011); David Welky, *Marching Across the Color Line: A. Philip Randolph and Civil Rights in the World War II Era* (New York: Oxford University Press, 2014).

3. Wynn, *African American Experience*.

4. Fraser M. Ottanelli, *The Communist Party of the United States: From the Depression to World War II* (New Brunswick, NJ: Rutgers University Press, 1991).

5. Andrew Edmund Kersten and Clarence Lang, eds., *Reframing Randolph: Labor, Black Freedom, and the Legacies of A. Philip Randolph* (New York: New York University Press, 2015); Bynum, *A. Philip Randolph*; Welky, *Marching Across the Color Line*.

6. Exec. Order No. 8802, 3 C.F.R. (1941).

7. William J. Collins, "Race, Roosevelt, and Wartime Production: Fair Employment in World War II Labor Markets," *American Economic Review* 91, no. 1 (March 2001), 272–86.

8. "Double Victory Democracy at Home—Abroad," *Pittsburgh Courier*, February 7, 1942, 1.

9. Roy Wilkins, "Yes, Negroes Know the Issues of War," *Crisis*, March 1942, 79.

10. Welky, *Marching Across the Color Line*.

11. Aldridge, *Becoming American*.

12. Bynum, *A. Philip Randolph*; Welky, *Marching Across the Color Line*.

13. Aldridge, *Becoming American*; Wynn, *African American Experience*.

14. Lynn M. Homan and Thomas Reilly, *Black Knights: The Story of the Tuskegee Airmen* (Gretna, LA: Pelican, 2002); Aldridge, *Becoming American*.

15. Samuel A. Stouffer, Edward A. Suchman, Leland C. DeVinney, Shirley A. Star, and Robin M. Williams Jr., *The American Soldier: Adjustment During Army Life*, volume I (Princeton, NJ: Princeton University Press, 1949), 492–94; Bell I. Wiley, *The Training of Negro Troops: Study No. 36* (Washington, DC: US Army Ground Forces, 1946), 7.

16. William Henry Chafe, *Civilities and Civil Rights: Greensboro, North Carolina, and the Black Struggle for Freedom* (1980; repr., New York: Oxford University Press,

1992); Raymond Arsenault, *Freedom Riders: 1961 and the Struggle for Racial Justice* (New York: Oxford University Press, 2011); Ann Bausum, *Freedom Riders: John Lewis and Jim Zwerg on the Front Lines of the Civil Rights Movement* (Washington, DC: National Geographic, 2006); Sullivan, *Lift Every Voice.*

17. James Farmer, *Lay Bare the Heart: An Autobiography of the Civil Rights Movement* (Fort Worth: Texas Christian University Press, 1998); Nishani Frazier, *Harambee City: The Congress of Racial Equality in Cleveland and the Rise of Black Power Populism* (Fayetteville: University of Arkansas Press, 2017); Inge Powell Bell, *CORE and the Strategy of Nonviolence* (New York: Random House, 1968).

18. John D'Emilio, *Lost Prophet: The Life and Times of Bayard Rustin* (Chicago: University of Chicago Press, 2004).

19. Sullivan, *Lift Every Voice.*

20. Sullivan, *Lift Every Voice.*

21. Sullivan, *Lift Every Voice.*

22. Committee on Civil Rights, *To Secure These Rights: The Report of the President's Committee on Civil Rights* (Washington, DC: US Government Printing Office, 1947).

23. Michael R. Gardner, *Harry Truman and Civil Rights: Moral Changes and Political Risks* (Carbondale: Southern Illinois University Press, 2002), 85.

24. Chris Mead, *Joe Louis: Black Champion in White America* (Mineola, NY: Dover, 2010); David Margolick, *Beyond Glory: Joe Louis vs. Max Schmeling, and a World on the Brink* (New York: Vintage, 2005).

25. Thomas R. Hietala, *The Fight of the Century: Jack Johnson, Joe Louis, and the Struggle for Racial Equality* (Armonk, NY: M. E. Sharpe, 2004); Randy Roberts, *Joe Louis: Hard Times Man* (New Haven, CT: Yale University Press, 2012).

26. Wendy L. Wall, *Inventing the "American Way": The Politics of Consensus from the New Deal to the Civil Rights Movement* (New York: Oxford University Press, 2008); Laurie B. Green, *Battling the Plantation Mentality: Memphis and the Black Freedom Struggle* (Chapel Hill: University of North Carolina Press, 2007).

27. Langston Hughes, "Freedom Train," *Our World,* October 1947, 26–27; Erik Christiansen, *Channeling the Past: Politicizing History in Postwar America* (Madison: University of Wisconsin Press, 2013).

28. Jeanne Theoharis, *The Rebellious Life of Mrs. Rosa Parks* (Boston: Beacon, 2015).

29. Stuart J. Little, "The Freedom Train: Citizenship and Postwar Political Culture, 1946–1949," *American Studies* 34, no. 1 (March 1, 1993): 35–67; John White, "Civil Rights in Conflict: The 'Birmingham Plan' and the Freedom Train, 1947," *Alabama Review* 52, no. 2 (April 1999); Vivian I. McMillan, "Freedom Train," *Chicago Defender,* February 14, 1948.

30. *The Documents on the Freedom Train* (New York: American Heritage Foundation, 1947).

31. "Freedom Train," The Hill Country Project, accessed March 18, 2018, http://www.hillcountryproject.org /the-freedom-train/.

Chapter Three

1. James T. Patterson, *Brown v. Board of Education: A Civil Rights Milestone and Its Troubled Legacy* (2001; repr., New York: Oxford University Press, 2010); Ben Keppel, *Brown v. Board and the Transformation of American Culture: Education and the South in the Age of Desegregation* (Baton Rouge: Louisiana State University Press, 2016); Richard Kluger, *Simple Justice: The History of Brown v. Board of Education and Black America's Struggle for Equality* (New York: Vintage, 2004).

2. *Brown v. Board of Education of Topeka,* 347 U.S. 483 (1954); Mark V. Tushnet, "'Our decision does not end but begins the struggle over segregation': Brown v. Board of Education, 1954, Justice Robert H. Jackson," in *I Dissent: Great Opposing Opinions in Landmark Supreme Court Cases* (Boston: Beacon, 2008), 133–50.

3. Brown v. Board of Education of Topeka, 349 U.S. 294 (1955); "The '*Brown II*' ('All Deliberate Speed') Decision (May 1954)," Civil Rights Movement Archive, accessed June 3, 2018, http://www.crmvet.org/tim/timhis55 .htm#1955ads.

4. *Griffin v. School Board,* 377 U.S. 218 (1964).

5. Devery S. Anderson, *Emmett Till: The Murder That Shocked the World and Propelled the Civil Rights Movement* (Jackson: University Press of Mississippi, 2017); Mamie Till-Mobley and Christopher Benson, *Death of Innocence: The Story of the Hate Crime That Changed America.* (New York: Ballantine, 2005).

6. Timothy B. Tyson, *The Blood of Emmett Till* (New York: Simon & Schuster, 2017); Jeanne Theoharis, *The Rebellious*

Life of Mrs. Rosa Parks (Boston: Beacon, 2015); Beth Loch, "Emmett Till's Legacy," Chicago Public Library, August 21, 2015, https://www.chipublib.org/blogs/post /emmett-tills-legacy-60-years-after-his-murder/.

7. Faith S. Holsaert et al., *Hands on the Freedom Plow: Personal Accounts by Women in SNCC* (Urbana: University of Illinois Press, 2012).

8. Diane McWhorter, "The Day Autherine Lucy Dared to Integrate the University of Alabama," *Journal of Blacks in Higher Education* 32 (Summer 2001); Howell Raines, *My Soul Is Rested: The Story of the Civil Rights Movement in the Deep South* (1977; repr., New York: Viking, 1988); Dwayne Mack, "Autherine Juanita Lucy (1929–)," BlackPast, accessed June 5, 2018, http://www.blackpast.org/aah /lucy-autherine-juanita-1929.

9. Jo Ann Robinson to Mayor W. A. Gayle, May 21, 1954, City Hall, Harriet St., Montgomery, Alabama; Jo Ann Gibson Robinson, *The Montgomery Bus Boycott and the Women Who Started It: The Memoir of Jo Ann Gibson Robinson* (1987; repr., Knoxville: University of Tennessee Press, 2011); Sullivan, *Lift Every Voice*; J. Mills Thornton, *Dividing Lines: Municipal Politics and the Struggle for Civil Rights in Montgomery, Birmingham, and Selma* (Tuscaloosa: University of Alabama Press, 2002).

10. Sullivan, *Lift Every Voice*; Ruth E. Martin, "Colvin, Claudette," in *The African American National Biography*, ed. Henry Louis Gates Jr. and Evelyn Brooks Higginbotham (2008; repr., New York: Oxford University Press, 2013); "Claudette Colvin: The First 'Rosa Parks,'" CORE, accessed June 5, 2018, http://www.core-online.org/History/colvin. htm; Taylor Branch, *Parting the Waters: America in the King Years, 1954–63* (1989; repr., New York: Simon and Schuster, 2006).

11. *Martin Luther King and the Montgomery Story* comic book (Nyack, NY: Fellowship of Reconciliation, 1957); Theoharis, *Rebellious Life*; J. Theoharis, "'I Don't Believe in Gradualism': Rosa Parks and the Black Power Movement in Detroit," paper presented at the 96th Annual Association for the Study of African American Life and History Conference: African Americans and the Civil War, Richmond, VA, October 5–9, 2011.

12. Theoharis, *Rebellious Life*; Joanne Grant, *Ella Baker: Freedom Bound* (New York: Wiley, 1999).

13. Robinson, *Montgomery Bus Boycott*; Llew Smith and Judy Richardson, "Interview with Jo Ann Robinson, August 27, 1979," *Eyes on the Prize I* interviews, http://digital.wustl .edu/e/eop/eopweb/rob0015.0530.090judyrichardson.html.

14. Branch, *Parting the Waters*; Gibson, *Montgomery Bus Boycott*; Aldon D. Morris, *The Origins of the Civil Rights Movement: Black Communities Organizing for Change* (New York: Free Press, 1986); Robert S. Graetz, *A White Preacher's Memoir: The Montgomery Bus Boycott* (Montgomery, AL: Black Belt Press, 1998).

15. Branch, *Parting the Waters*.

16. Sullivan, *Lift Every Voice*.

17. Andrew M. Manis, *A Fire You Can't Put Out: The Civil Rights Life of Birmingham's Reverend Fred Shuttlesworth* (1999; repr., Tuscaloosa: University of Alabama Press, 2002).

18. Branch, *Parting the Waters*; Gibson, *Montgomery Bus Boycott*.

19. William L. Van Deburg, ed., *Modern Black Nationalism: From Marcus Garvey to Louis Farrakhan* (New York: New York University Press, 1997); Dean E. Robinson, *Black Nationalism in American Politics and Thought* (2001; repr., New York: Cambridge University Press, 2006).

20. "The Alabama Christian Movement for Human Rights," Stanford University, Martin Luther King, Jr. Research and Education Institute, Martin Luther King, Jr. Encyclopedia, accessed June 6, 2018, https://kinginstitute.stanford.edu /encyclopedia/alabama-christian-movement-human -rights-acmhr; Branch, *Parting the Waters*.

21. Karen Anderson, *Little Rock: Race and Resistance at Central High School* (2010; repr., Princeton, NJ: Princeton University Press, 2014); Carlotta Walls LaNier with Lisa Frazier Page, *A Mighty Long Way: My Journey to Justice at Little Rock Central High School* (New York: One World Trade, 2010).

Chapter Four

1. Taylor Branch, *Pillar of Fire: America in the King Years, 1963–65* (New York: Simon & Schuster, 1999); Branch, *Parting the Waters*; Sullivan, *Lift Every Voice;* Verney and Sartain, *Long Is the Way;* Christopher Waldrep, *African Americans Confront Lynching: Strategies of Resistance from the Civil War to the Civil Rights Era* (Lanham, MD: Rowman & Littlefield, 2008).

2. Chafe, *Civilities and Civil Rights*; Iwan Morgan and Philip Davies, eds., *From Sit-Ins to SNCC: The Student Civil Rights Movement in the 1960s* (Gainesville: University Press of Florida, 2013); M. J. O'Brien, *We Shall Not Be Moved: The Jackson Woolworth's Sit-In and the Movement It Inspired* (Jackson: University Press of Mississippi, 2014).

3. "Sit-in Nation," International Civil Rights Center & Museum, accessed June 20, 2017, https://www.sitinmovement.org/sit-in-nation; "Sit-ins Sweep across the South (1960–1964)," Civil Rights Movement Archive, https://www.crmvet.org/tim/timhis60.htm#1960sitins; Melody Herr, *Sitting for Equal Service: Lunch Counter Sit-Ins, United States, 1960s* (Minneapolis: Twenty-First Century Books, 2011); Juan Williams with the *Eyes on the Prize* Production Team, *Eyes on the Prize: America's Civil Rights Years, 1954–1965* (New York: Penguin, 1988); Miles Wolff, *Lunch at the 5 & 10* (Chicago: I. R. Dee, 1990).

4. Howard Zinn, *SNCC: The New Abolitionists* (Chicago: Haymarket, 2013); Grant, *Ella Baker*; Christina Greene, *Our Separate Ways: Women and the Black Freedom Movement in Durham, North Carolina* (Chapel Hill: University of North Carolina Press, 2005); Holsaert et al., *Hands on the Freedom Plow*; J. Todd Moye, *Ella Baker: Community Organizer of the Civil Rights Movement* (Lanham, MD: Rowman & Littlefield, 2015).

5. Yvonne Ryan, *Roy Wilkins: The Quiet Revolutionary and the NAACP* (Lexington: University of Kentucky Press, 2014).

6. *Boynton v. Virginia*, 364 U.S. 454 (1960); Arsenault, *Freedom Riders*; Bausum, *Freedom Riders*; Lisa Mullins, *Diane Nash: The Fire of the Civil Rights Movement: A Biography* (Miami: Barnhardt & Ashe, 2007).

7. Derek Charles Catsam, *Freedom's Main Line: The Journey of Reconciliation and the Freedom Rides* (Lexington: University Press of Kentucky, 2011); Thomas M. Armstrong and Natalie R. Bell, *Autobiography of a Freedom Rider: My Life as a Foot Soldier for Civil Rights* (Deerfield Beach, FL: Health Communications, 2011).

8. Eric Etheridge, *Breach of Peace: Portraits of the 1961 Mississippi Freedom Riders* (New York: Atlas, 2008); "Freedom Riders," *American Experience*, written, produced, and directed by Stanley Nelson, aired May 16, 2011, on PBS; Arsenault, *Freedom Riders*; Bausum, *Freedom Riders*; Mullins, *Diane Nash*.

9. "Oral History Interview with Laurie Pritchett, April 23, 1976," interview by James Reston Jr., Southern Oral History Program Collection (#4007), http://docsouth.unc.edu/sohp/B-0027/menu.html. Laurie Pritchett was the chief of police for Albany, Georgia, during the Albany Movement. His efforts stifled the protests and frustrated civil rights organizations. Mary F. Jenkins, *Open Dem Cells: A Pictorial History of the Albany Movement* (Columbus, GA: Brentwood Academic Press, 2000).

10. William T. Martin Riches, *The Civil Rights Movement: Struggle and Resistance* (London: Palgrave Macmillan, 2004), 67–68.

11. Bernice Johnson Reagon, "The Freedom Singers" (lecture presented at Looking Back, Moving Forward: 50th Anniversary Commemoration of the Civil Rights Movement 1964–2014, Syracuse University, Syracuse, NY, March 21, 2014); Deanna Frith Weber, "The Freedom Singers: Their History and Legacy for Music Education" (PhD diss., Boston University, 2010); Reiland Rabaka, *Civil Rights Music: The Soundtracks of the Civil Rights Movement* (Lanham, MD: Lexington Books, 2016); Martin Luther King Jr., *The Autobiography of Martin Luther King, Jr.*, ed. Clayborne Carson (2001; repr., London: Abacus, 2006).

12. "More Than a Documentary: Freedom in the Air 'An Inspiring Album,' Says Chronicle," *Student Voice* (Atlanta) 3, no. 3 (October 1962), 3, http://www.crmvet.org/docs/sv/sv6210.pdf.

13. Tullia Brown Hamilton, *Up from Canaan: The African American Journey from Mound Bayou to St. Louis* (St. Louis, MO: PenUltimate, 2011); Charles M. Payne, *I've Got the Light of Freedom: The Organizing Tradition and the Mississippi Freedom Struggle* (Berkeley: University of California Press, 2007); John Dittmer, *Local People: The Struggle for Civil Rights in Mississippi* (1995; repr., Urbana: University of Illinois Press, 2006); David T. Beito and Linda Royster Beito, *Black Maverick: T. R. M. Howard's Fight for Civil Rights and Economic Power* (Urbana: University of Illinois Press, 2009).

14. "Smithsonian Prepares Civil Rights–Era Artifacts," *All Things Considered*, NPR, April 3, 2011, https://www.npr.org/2011/04/03/135092962/black-museums-latest-finds-klan-rally-drumsticks. National Museum of African American History and Culture director Lonnie Bunch described a "denim vest with SNCC buttons" and a "never" pinback upside down.

15. Michael Vinson Williams, *Medgar Evers: Mississippi Martyr* (Fayetteville: University of Arkansas Press, 2013); Adam Nossiter, *Of Long Memory: Mississippi and the Murder of Medgar Evers* (Cambridge, MA: Da Capo, 2002); Myrlie Evers-Williams with William Peters, *For Us, the Living* (1967; repr., Jackson: University Press of Mississippi, 1996).

16. Sullivan, *Lift Every Voice*; Payne, *I've Got the Light*; Charles Evers, *Evers* (New York: World Publishing, 1971).

17. Leonard N. Moore, *Carl B. Stokes and the Rise of Black Political Power* (Urbana: University of Illinois Press, 2003).

18. Frazier, *Harambee City*.

19. Moore, *Carl B. Stokes*; David Stradling and Richard Stradling, *Where the River Burned: Carl Stokes and the Struggle to Save Cleveland* (Ithaca, NY: Cornell University Press, 2015).

20. Bynum, *A. Philip Randolph*; Sullivan, *Lift Every Voice*; Troy Jackson, *Becoming King: Martin Luther King Jr. and the Making of a National Leader* (Lexington: University Press of Kentucky, 2011); Exec. Order No. 8802, 3 C.F.R. (1941).

21. Glenn T. Eskew, *But for Birmingham: The Local and National Movements in the Civil Rights Struggle* (1997; repr., Chapel Hill: University of North Carolina Press, 2000); Branch, *Parting the Waters*; Diane McWhorter, *Carry Me Home: Birmingham, Alabama, the Climactic Battle of the Civil Rights Revolution* (New York: Simon & Schuster, 2013).

22. Branch, *Pillar of Fire*; Taylor Branch, *At Canaan's Edge: America in the King Years, 1965–68* (New York: Simon & Schuster, 2006); Branch, *Parting the Waters*; Bynum, *A. Philip Randolph*; D'Emilio, *Lost Prophet*.

23. Bynum, *A. Philip Randolph*.

24. Verney and Sartain, *Long Is the Way*; Clayborne Carson, *In Struggle: SNCC and the Black Awakening of the 1960s* (1995; repr., Cambridge, MA: Harvard University Press, 2001).

25. Grant, *Ella Baker*; Holsaert et al., *Hands on the Freedom Plow*; Kay Mills, *This Little Light of Mine: The Life of Fannie Lou Hamer* (Lexington: University Press of Kentucky, 2007); Moye, *Ella Baker*; Mullins, *Diane Nash*.

26. Gloster B. Current, "58th Annual NAACP Convention: National Nominating Committee," *Crisis*, August–September 1967, 360; Henry Lee Moon, ed., "Battlefront: Membership Renewals Sought in Campaign," *Crisis*, December 1970, 411.

27. John Lewis with Michael D'Orso, *Walking with the Wind: A Memoir of the Movement* (New York: Simon & Schuster, 2015), 227; Mullins, *Diane Nash*.

28. Bynum, *A. Philip Randolph*; D'Emilio, *Lost Prophet*.

29. Cleveland Robinson and Bayard Rustin, "Final Plans for the March on Washington for Jobs and Freedom: Organizing Manual No. 2" (New York: March on Washington for Jobs and Freedom, 1963), http://www.crmvet.org/docs/moworg2.pdf.

30. Congressman John Lewis, phone conversation with author, June 26, 2014.

31. Leonard Freed and Michael Eric Dyson, *This Is the Day: The March on Washington* (Los Angeles: J. Paul Getty Museum, 2013); Jervis Anderson, *Bayard Rustin: Troubles I've Seen; A Biography* (Berkeley: University of California Press, 1998); William P. Jones, *The March on Washington: Jobs, Freedom, and the Forgotten History of Civil Rights* (New York: W. W. Norton, 2014).

32. The Leadership Conference on Civil Rights and the March on Washington for Jobs and Freedom, *Call for a National Campaign for a Strong Civil Rights Bill by Christmas* (New York: Leadership Conference on Civil Rights and March on Washington for Jobs and Freedom, 1963).

33. Jon N. Hale, *The Freedom Schools: Student Activists in the Mississippi Civil Rights Movement* (New York: Columbia University Press, 2016); William Sturkey and Jon N. Hale, eds., *To Write in the Light of Freedom: The Newspapers of the 1964 Mississippi Freedom Schools* (Jackson: University Press of Mississippi, 2015).

34. Hale, *Freedom Schools*; Sturkey and Hale, *To Write in the Light*.

35. Mammoth Life and Accident Insurance Company, "March on Frankfurt Souvenir Program," Lexington, KY, 1964; Thomas McAdam, "The Day I Met Martin Luther King," *Louisville Magazine*, January 18, 2016, http://www.ilocalnews.com/louisville-parkland/day-i-met-martin-luther-king.

36. Mammoth Life and Accident Insurance Company, "March on Frankfurt Souvenir Program."

37. Southern Student Organizing Committee, "Founding Prospectus," news release, Civil Rights Movement Archive, accessed June 29, 2017, https://www.crmvet.org/docs/64_ssoc_about.pdf.

38. Southern Student Organizing Committee brochure, 1964, accessed June 29, 2017, https://www.crmvet.org /docs/64_ssoc_brochure.pdf.

39. Alan B. Anderson and George W. Pickering, *Confronting the Color Line: The Broken Promise of the Civil Rights Movement in Chicago* (Athens: University of Georgia Press, 1986).

40. Clay Risen, *The Bill of the Century: The Epic Battle for the Civil Rights Act* (New York: Bloomsbury, 2015); Todd S. Purdum, *An Idea Whose Time Has Come: Two Presidents, Two Parties, and the Battle for the Civil Rights Act of 1964* (New York: Picador, 2015).

41. Civil Rights Act of 1964, 352, 88 Cong., 241 U.S. Statutes at Large 78 (1964) (enacted).

42. Dittmer, *Local People*; Beito and Beito, *Black Maverick*; Payne, *I've Got the Light.*

43. Branch, *Pillar of Fire*; Branch, *Parting the Waters.*

44. Thornton, *Dividing Lines.*

45. Eric Burner, *And Gently He Shall Lead Them: Robert Parris Moses and Civil Rights in Mississippi* (New York: New York University Press, 1994).

46. William J. Boerst, *Marching in Birmingham* (Greensboro, NC: Morgan Reynolds, 2008); Richie Jean Sherrod Jackson, *The House by the Side of the Road: The Selma Civil Rights Movement* (Tuscaloosa: University of Alabama Press, 2011); Nicolaus Mills, *Like a Holy Crusade: Mississippi 1964—The Turning of the Civil Rights Movement in America* (Chicago: I. R. Dee, 1993).

47. Seth Cagin and Philip Dray, *We Are Not Afraid: The Story of Goodman, Schwerner, and Chaney, and the Civil Rights Campaign for Mississippi* (New York: Macmillan, 1988).

48. James Farmer, *Calendar of Coercion* (New York: Congress of Racial Equality, 1964).

49. Farmer, *Calendar of Coercion.*

50. Mills, *This Little Light;* Grant, *Ella Baker.*

51. Mills, *This Little Light.*

52. Willy Siegel Leventhal, *The SCOPE of Freedom: The Leadership of Hosea Williams with Dr. King's Summer '65 Student Volunteers* (Montgomery, AL: Challenge, 2005).

53. Southern Christian Leadership Conference, "The Summer Community Organization and Political Education Project of the Southern Christian Leadership Conference," news release, Civil Rights Movement Archive, accessed June 29, 2017, http://www.crmvet.org/docs/65_sclc_ scope.pdf.

54. "Purpose of SCLC's Summer Community Organization and Political Education (SCOPE) Project," Southern Christian Leadership Conference, Political Education and Voter Registration Department, Summer Community Organization and Political Education Project, May 1965, Civil Rights Movement Archive, http://www.crmvet.org /docs/65_scope_handout.pdf.

55. "Recruiting," SCOPE Project to Southern Christian Leadership Conference, May 1965, Civil Rights Movement Archive, http://www.crmvet.org/docs/65_scope_ recruiting.pdf.

56. "Instructions," Hosea L. Williams to SCOPE Workers, June 1965, Civil Rights Movement Archive, http://www .crmvet.org/docs/65_scope_memo1.pdf.

57. "SCOPE for 1966," Hosea L. Williams to Southern Christian Leadership Conference's Summer Community Organization and Political Education Project Volunteers, October 1965, Civil Rights Movement Archive, http://www .crmvet.org/docs/66_scope.pdf.

58. Congressman John Lewis, phone conversation with author, June, 26 2014. Lewis and D'Orso, *Walking with the Wind.*

59. Robert A. Pratt, *Selma's Bloody Sunday: Protest, Voting Rights, and the Struggle for Racial Equality* (Baltimore: Johns Hopkins University Press, 2017); David Aretha, *Freedom Summer* (Greensboro, NC: Morgan Reynolds, 2008); David Aretha, *The Story of the Selma Voting Rights Marches in Photographs* (Berkeley Heights, NJ: Enslow, 2014).

60. Horace Julian Bond, interview by author, Martin Luther King, Jr. National Historical Park, Atlanta, May 10, 2014.

61. "Voting Rights Act of 1965" (PL 89-110, August 6, 1965), 79, *United States Statutes at Large*, 437–46, http://www.gpo .gov/fdsys/pkg/STATUTE-79/pdf/STATUTE-79-Pg437. pdf. It should be mentioned that in *Shelby County v. Holder* (2013), the US Supreme Court ruled that the formula in section 4 was unconstitutional because it singled out states with a history of Jim Crow practices, rather than applying to all states; *Shelby County v. Holder*, 570 U.S. 529 (2013).

62. Gabriel Jackson Chin and Lori Wagner, *U.S. Commission on Civil Rights: Reports on Voting* (Getzville, NY: William S. Hein & Co., 2005), https://ssrn.com/abstract=268118.

Chapter Five
——

1. Daniel S. Lucks, *Selma to Saigon: The Civil Rights Movement and the Vietnam War* (Lexington: University Press of Kentucky, 2017); Jonathan Rosenberg, *How Far the Promised Land?: World Affairs and the American Civil Rights Movement from the First World War to Vietnam* (Princeton, NJ: Princeton University Press, 2006).

2. Mary Lou Finley, Bernard LaFayette Jr., James R. Ralph Jr., and Pam Smith, eds., *The Chicago Freedom Movement: Martin Luther King Jr. and Civil Rights Activism in the North* (Lexington: University Press of Kentucky, 2018).

3. Lawrence S. Wittner, *Working for Peace and Justice: Memoirs of an Activist Intellectual* (Knoxville: University of Tennessee Press, 2012); Simon Hall, *Peace and Freedom: The Civil Rights and Antiwar Movements of the 1960s* (Philadelphia: University of Pennsylvania Press, 2006).

4. Eldridge Cleaver, *Soul on Ice* (New York: McGraw-Hill, 1968).

5. Dick Gregory and James R. McGraw, *Write Me In!* (New York: Bantam Books, 1968); Dick Gregory with Sheila P. Moses, *Callus on My Soul: A Memoir* (New York: Dafina, 2003); Darcy G. Richardson, *A Nation Divided: The 1968 Presidential Campaign* (Lincoln, NE: Writers Club, 2002).

6. Charles Evers and Andrew Szanton, *Have No Fear: The Charles Evers Story* (New York: Wiley, 1998); Jason Berry, *Amazing Grace: With Charles Evers in Mississippi* (New York: Saturday Review Press, 1978); Williams, *Medgar Evers*; Evers, *Evers*.

7. Nossiter, *Of Long Memory*; Williams, *Medgar Evers*; Medgar Evers, *The Autobiography of Medgar Evers: A Hero's Life and Legacy Revealed through His Writings, Letters, and Speeches*, ed. Myrlie Evers-Williams and Manning Marable (New York: Basic Civitas, 2006); Beito and Beito, *Black Maverick*.

8. Evers and Szanton, *Have No Fear*; Emilye Crosby, *A Little Taste of Freedom: The Black Freedom Struggle in Claiborne County, Mississippi* (Chapel Hill: University of North Carolina Press, 2005); Moore, *Carl B. Stokes*.

9. Charles George, *Civil Rights: The Struggle for Black Equality* (San Diego, CA: Lucent, 2001); Anderson, *Emmett Till*; Sullivan, *Lift Every Voice*.

10. Howard O. Robinson, "Rev. Richard Charles Boone," *Alabama Heritage* 113 (Summer 2014), https://www.alabamaheritage.com/issue-113-summer-2014.html; Sandra Colvin and Robin Reisig, "Black Christmas," *Southern Courier* (Montgomery, AL) 3, no. 53, December 30, 1967, http://www.southerncourier.org/low-res/Vol3_No53_1967_12_30.pdf.

11. Robinson, "Rev. Richard Charles Boone."

12. Emilie Raymond, *Stars for Freedom: Hollywood, Black Celebrities, and the Civil Rights Movement* (Seattle: University of Washington Press, 2018).

13. Anne L. Durrah and Carole F. Hoover, *Stars for Freedom* (Atlanta: Diamond Printing Company, 1967)

14. Durrah and Hoover, *Stars for Freedom*.

15. Aretha, *Freedom Summer*; Pratt, *Selma's Bloody Sunday*.

16. Raymond, *Stars for Freedom*; Dan McQuade, "MLK Speaks at Philadelphia Middle School in 1967." *Philadelphia Magazine*, January 18, 2016, https://www.phillymag.com/news/2016/01/18/mlk-speaks-philadelphia-middle-school/.

17. SCLC Staff, *SCLC Project Report* (Atlanta: Southern Christian Leadership Conference, 1967); David J. Garrow, *Bearing the Cross: Martin Luther King, Jr., and the Southern Christian Leadership Conference* (New York: William Morrow, 2004).

18. Garrow, *Bearing the Cross*.

19. Sullivan, *Lift Every Voice*.

20. *NAACP: Celebrating a Century; 100 Years in Pictures* (Layton, UT: Gibbs Smith, 2009).

21. *NAACP: Celebrating a Century*; *Griggs v. Duke Power Co.*, 401 U.S. 424 (1971).

22. Roy Wilkins, *The State of the NAACP* (New York: National Association for the Advancement of Colored People, 1969); Elliot Rudwick and August Meier, "Organizational Structure and Goal Succession: A Comparative Analysis of the NAACP and CORE, 1964–1968," *Social Science Quarterly* 51, no. 1 (June 1970): 9–24, https://www.jstor.org/stable/42858539?seq=1#pagescantabcontents.

23. Hall, *Peace and Freedom*; Rosenberg, *How Far the Promised Land*.

24. Kenneth Robert Janken, *The Wilmington Ten: Violence, Injustice, and the Rise of Black Politics in the 1970s* (Chapel Hill: University of North Carolina Press, 2015); Timothy B. Tyson, *Blood Done Sign My Name* (New York: Crown, 2004); Wayne Moore, *Triumphant Warrior: A Soul Survivor of the Wilmington Ten* (Ann Arbor, MI: Warrior Press, 2014); *Chavis v. State of North Carolina*, 637 F.2d 213 (4th Cir. 1980); Elissa Auther and Adam Lerner, eds., *West of Center:*

Art and the Counterculture Experiment in America, 1965–1977 (Minneapolis: University of Minnesota Press, 2012).

25. Michael W. Flamm, "'Law and Order' at Large: The New York Civilian Review Board Referendum of 1966 and the Crisis of Liberalism," *Historian* 64, no. 3/4 (Spring–Summer 2002): 643–65, http://www.jstor.org/stable/24451025.

26. Minnie Bruce Pratt, "Lowndes County, Alabama: 'The Original Black Panther Party,'" *Workers World*, March 30, 2016, https://www.workers.org/2016/03/24664/; Hasan Kwame Jeffries, *Bloody Lowndes: Civil Rights and Black Power in Alabama's Black Belt* (New York: New York University Press, 2010); "Lowndes County Freedom Organization," BlackPast, accessed August 19, 2018, http://www.blackpast.org/aah/lowndes-county-freedom-organization.

27. Lincoln Cushing, "The Women Behind the Black Panther Party Logo," Docs Populi, February 1, 2018, https://www.docspopuli.org/articles/BlackPantherPartyLogo.html.

28. Dorothy Zellner, email reproduced in "The Black Panther Symbol: An Email Discussion, May–June 2006," Veterans of the Civil Rights Movement, June 2, 2006, http://www.crmvet.org/disc/panther.htm; Cushing, "Women Behind the Black Panther Party Logo"; "Roadside Sign for the Lowndes County Freedom Organization: Jim Peppler Southern Courier Photograph Collection," Alabama Department of Archives and History, Montgomery, accessed August 19, 2018, http://digital.archives.alabama.gov/cdm/ref/collection/peppler/id/1867.

29. Pratt, "Lowndes County, Alabama."

30. Cushing, "Women Behind the Black Panther Party Logo."

31. "Lowndes County Freedom Organization"; Clayborne Carson, *In Struggle: SNCC and the Black Awakening of the 1960s* (Cambridge, MA: Harvard University Press, 1981).

32. Peniel E. Joseph, ed., *The Black Power Movement: Rethinking the Civil Rights–Black Power Era* (Oxfordshire: Taylor and Francis, 2013); Jama Lazerow and Yohuru Williams, eds., *In Search of the Black Panther Party: New Perspectives on a Revolutionary Movement* (Durham, NC: Duke University Press, 2007); Hugh Pearson, *The Shadow of the Panther: Huey Newton and the Price of Black Power in America* (Cambridge, MA: Perseus, 2012).

33. Pearson, *Shadow of the Panther*.

34. Cleaver, *Soul on Ice*.

35. Joseph, *Black Power Movement*; Lazerow and Williams, *In Search of the Black Panther Party*.

36. Joseph, *Black Power Movement*; Lazerow and Williams, *In Search of the Black Panther Party*.

37. Lance Hill, *The Deacons for Defense: Armed Resistance and the Civil Rights Movement* (Chapel Hill: University of North Carolina Press, 2006); Eldridge Cleaver for President Committee, Peace and Freedom Party, Black Panther Party, May 13, 1968, "The Black Panther," news release, Freedom Archives, http://freedomarchives.org/Documents/Finder/DOC513_scans/Eldridge%20Cleaver/513.E.CLEAVER.cleaver.for.pres.may.13.1968.pdf.

38. Allen Barra, "The Integration of College Football Didn't Happen in One Game," *Atlantic*, November 15, 2013, https://www.theatlantic.com/entertainment/archive/2013/11/the-integration-of-college-football-didnt-happen-in-one-game/281557/.

39. Paul C. Bermanzohn and Sally A. Bermanzohn, *The True Story of the Greensboro Massacre* (New York: César Cauce, 1980); Elizabeth Wheaton, *Codename GREENKIL: The 1979 Greensboro Killings* (Athens: University of Georgia Press, 2009).

40. "Death to the Klan" flyer, Civil Rights Greensboro, UNC-Greensboro Digital Collections, accessed August 19, 2018, http://libcdm1.uncg.edu/cdm/compoundobject/collection/CivilRights/id/100/rec/9; "Come to Greensboro to Join a New Movement for Justice" flyer, Civil Rights Greensboro, UNC-Greensboro Digital Collections, accessed August 19, 2018, http://libcdm1.uncg.edu/cdm/compoundobject/collection/CivilRights/id/303/rec/19; "Free Nelson Johnson and the Greensboro 3" flyer, Civil Rights Greensboro, UNC-Greensboro Digital Collections, accessed August 19, 2018, http://libcdm1.uncg.edu/cdm/compoundobject/collection/CivilRights/id/375/rec/20; "Who Are the Greensboro Three?" flyer, Civil Rights Greensboro, UNC-Greensboro Digital Collections, accessed August 19, 2018, http://libcdm1.uncg.edu/cdm/singleitem/collection/CivilRights/id/182/rec/15.

41. Stradling and Stradling, *Where the River Burned*; Moore, *Carl B. Stokes*.

42. Richardson, *A Nation Divided*; Lewis L. Gould, *1968: The Election That Changed America* (Chicago: Ivan R. Dee, 1993); *NAACP: Celebrating a Century*.

43. Burton Ira Kaufman, *The Carter Years* (New York: Facts on File, 2006); Ronald B. Walters, *Black Presidential Politics in America: A Strategic Approach* (Albany: State University of New York Press, 1988).

44. Walters, *Black Presidential Politics in America.*

45. Cedric Johnson, *Revolutionaries to Race Leaders: Black Power and the Making of African American Politics* (Minneapolis: University of Minnesota Press, 2007); "National Black Conferences and National Black Assembly," in *The Black Power Movement, Part 1: Amiri Baraka, from Black Arts to Black Radicalism*, ed. Komozi Woodard, Randolph Boehm, and Daniel Lewis (Bethesda, MD: University Publications of America, 2000), microfilm, reel 3, series 6; Cook, *Deacons for Defense.*

46. Bruce M. Tyler, "The Rise and Decline of the Watts Summer Festival, 1965 to 1986," *American Studies* 31, no. 2 (Fall 1990): 61–81, https://www.jstor.org/ stable/40642389?seq=1#page_scan_tab_contents; Robert Bauman, "Watts Summer Festival, Los Angeles (1966–)," BlackPast, March 18, 2010, http://www.blackpast.org/aaw /watts-summer-festival-1966; Elwood Watson, "Stephanie St. Clair (1897–1969), BlackPast, February 13, 2008, https://www.blackpast.org/african-american-history/ st-clair-stephanie-1886-1969/.

47. John A. Kirk, ed., *Martin Luther King, Jr. and the Civil Rights Movement: Controversies and Debates* (Basingstoke, UK: Palgrave Macmillan, 2007); "When Jesus Says Love He Means It: Excerpts from Martin Luther King Jr.'s 1967 Frogmore Speech on Its 50th Anniversary," Kairos, September 27, 2017, https://kairoscenter.org/ mlk-frogmore-staff-retreat-speech-anniversary/; Gordon Keith Mantler, *Power to the Poor: Black-Brown Coalition and the Fight for Economic Justice, 1960–1974* (Chapel Hill: University of North Carolina Press, 2013).

48. Michael K. Honey, *Going Down Jericho Road: The Memphis Strike, Martin Luther King's Last Campaign* (New York: W. W. Norton, 2008).

49. Honey, *Going Down Jericho Road*; Clay Risen, *A Nation on Fire: America in the Wake of the King Assassination* (Hoboken, NJ: John Wiley & Sons, 2009); Gerald D. McKnight, *The Last Crusade: Martin Luther King, Jr., the FBI, and the Poor People's Campaign* (Boulder, CO: Westview Press, 1998).

50. "Veterans of the Civil Rights Movement—Economic Bill of Rights," Veterans of the Civil Rights Movement— Charles Person, accessed August 25, 2018, http://www. crmvet.org/docs/68ebr.htm; McKnight, *Last Crusade*; Mantler, *Power to the Poor.*

51. Jill Freedman, *Old News: Resurrection City* (New York: Grossman, 1970); "About the Poor People's Campaign: A National Call for Moral Revival," Poor People's Campaign, accessed August 25, 2018, https://www .poorpeoplescampaign.org/history/.

52. Anna Diamond, "Remembering Resurrection City and the Poor People's Campaign of 1968," *Smithsonian*, May 2018, https://www.smithsonianmag.com/history/ remembering-poor-peoples-campaign-180968742/.

53. McKnight, *Last Crusade*; Mantler, *Power to the Poor.*

54. "The 15 Year Battle for Martin Luther King, Jr. Day," National Museum of African American History and Culture, https://nmaahc.si.edu/ blog-post/15-year-battle-martin-luther-king-jr-day.

55. Jill Hambert, Paul Booth, Mimi Feingold, and Carl Wittman, *Where It's At: A Research Guide for Community Organizing* (Boston: New England Free Press, 1967).

56. Sundiata Djata, *Blacks at the Net: Black Achievement in the History of Tennis* (Syracuse, NY: Syracuse University Press, 2006); Zirin, Dave. *Jim Brown: Last Man Standing* (New York: Penguin Publishing Group, 2018).

57. Joseph, *Black Power Movement*; Lazerow and Williams, *In Search of the Black Panther Party*; Pearson, *Shadow of the Panther.*

SELECTED BIBLIOGRAPHY

Ackerman, Lillian A., ed. *A Song to the Creator: Traditional Arts of Native American Women of the Plateau.* Norman: University of Oklahoma Press, 1996.

Aretha, David. *The Story of the Selma Voting Rights Marches in Photographs.* Berkeley Heights, NJ: Enslow, 2014.

Auther, Elissa, and Adam Lerner, eds. *West of Center: Art and the Counterculture Experiment in America, 1965–1977.* Minneapolis: University of Minnesota Press, 2012.

Berger, Maurice. *For All the World to See: Visual Culture and the Struggle for Civil Rights.* New Haven, CT: Yale University Press, 2010.

Bertens, Hans. *The Idea of the Postmodern: A History.* London: Routledge, 1996.

Bleichmar, Daniela, and Peter C. Mancall, eds. *Collecting Across Cultures: Material Exchanges in the Early Modern Atlantic World.* Philadelphia: University of Pennsylvania Press, 2013.

Branch, Taylor. *At Canaan's Edge: America in the King Years, 1965–68.* New York: Simon & Schuster, 2006. *Parting the Waters: America in the King Years, 1954–63.* 1989; repr., New York: Simon & Schuster, 2006. *Pillar of Fire: America in the King Years, 1963–65.* New York: Simon & Schuster, 1999.

Bronner, Simon J. *Grasping Things: Folk Material Culture and Mass Society in America.* Lexington: University Press of Kentucky, 2004.

Brooks, Alasdair, ed. *The Importance of British Material Culture to Historical Archaeologies of the Nineteenth Century.* Lincoln: University of Nebraska Press, 2016.

Carawan, Guy, and Candie Carawan, eds. *Sing for Freedom: The Story of the Civil Rights Movement through Its Songs.* Montgomery, AL: New South Books, 2007.

Carr, David. *Time, Narrative, and History.* 1991; repr., Bloomington: Indiana University Press, 1999.

Cleaver, Eldridge. *Soul on Ice.* New York: McGraw-Hill, 1968.

Cobb, Charles E., Jr. *This Nonviolent Stuff'll Get You Killed: How Guns Made the Civil Rights Movement Possible.* Durham, NC: Duke University Press, 2016.

Craven, Anna. "The Art and Material Culture of the Eloyi (Afo) People, Nigeria 1969/70: A Photographic Essay." *African Arts* 51, no. 1 (Spring 2018): 46–63. https://doi.org/10.1162/AFAR_a_00391.

Egerton, John. *Speak Now Against the Day: The Generation Before the Civil Rights Movement in the South.* Chapel Hill: University of North Carolina Press, 1995.

Farmer, James. *Lay Bare the Heart: An Autobiography of the Civil Rights Movement.* Fort Worth: Texas Christian University Press, 1998.

Gerhart, Karen M. *The Material Culture of Death in Medieval Japan.* Honolulu: University of Hawaii Press, 2009.

Graetz, Robert S. *A White Preacher's Memoir: The Montgomery Bus Boycott.* Montgomery, AL: Black Belt Press, 1998.

Greene, Christina. *Our Separate Ways: Women and the Black Freedom Movement in Durham, North Carolina.* Chapel Hill: University of North Carolina Press, 2005.

Greenhaw, Wayne. *Fighting the Devil in Dixie: How Civil Rights Activists Took on the Ku Klux Klan in Alabama.* 2011; repr., Chicago: Lawrence Hill Books, 2015.

Gregory, Dick, and James R. McGraw. *Write Me In!.* New York: Bantam Books, 1968.

Heneghan, Bridget T. *Whitewashing America: Material Culture and Race in the Antebellum Imagination.* Jackson: University Press of Mississippi, 2003.

Hill, Lance. *The Deacons for Defense: Armed Resistance and the Civil Rights Movement.* Chapel Hill: University of North Carolina Press, 2006.

Holsaert, Faith S., Martha Prescod Norman Noonan, Judy Richardson, Betty Garman Robinson, Jean Smith Young, and Dorothy M. Zellner, eds. *Hands on the Freedom Plow: Personal Accounts by Women in SNCC*. Urbana: University of Illinois Press, 2012.

Jeffries, Hasan Kwame. *Bloody Lowndes: Civil Rights and Black Power in Alabama's Black Belt*. New York: New York University Press, 2010.

Lewis, John, with Michael D'Orso. *Walking with the Wind: A Memoir of the Movement*. New York: Simon & Schuster, 2015.

Lyon, Danny. *Memories of the Southern Civil Rights Movement*. Santa Fe, NM: Twin Palms, 2010.

Lyotard, Jean-François. *The Differend: Phrases in Dispute*. Translated by Georges Van Den Abbeele. 1989; repr., Minneapolis: University of Minnesota Press, 2007. *The Postmodern Condition: A Report on Knowledge*. Translated by Geoff Bennington and Brian Massumi. 1984 [1979]; repr., Minneapolis: University of Minnesota Press, 1997.

Manis, Andrew M. *A Fire You Can't Put Out: The Civil Rights Life of Birmingham's Reverend Fred Shuttlesworth*. 1999; repr., Tuscaloosa: University of Alabama Press, 2002.

Moses, Wilson Jeremiah. *The Golden Age of Black Nationalism, 1850–1925*. 1978; repr., New York: Oxford University Press, 2009.

Mullins, Paul R. *Race and Affluence: An Archaeology of African America and Consumer Culture*. Boston: Springer US, 2002.

Nahal, Anita, and Lopez D. Matthews Jr. "African American Women and the Niagara Movement, 1905–1909." *Afro-Americans in New York Life and History* 32, no. 2 (July 2008).

Patterson, James T. *Brown v. Board of Education: A Civil Rights Milestone and Its Troubled Legacy*. 2001; repr., New York: Oxford University Press, 2010.

Pierce, Elizabeth, Anthony Russell, Adrián Maldonado, and Louisa Campbell, eds. *Creating Material Worlds: The Uses of Identity in Archaeology*. Oxford: Oxbow Books, 2016.

Pilgrim, David. *Watermelons, Nooses, and Straight Razors: Stories from the Jim Crow Museum*. Oakland, CA: PM Press, 2018.

Provenzo, Eugene F., Jr. *W. E. B. Du Bois's Exhibit of American Negroes: African Americans at the Beginning of the Twentieth Century*. Lanham, MD: Rowman & Littlefield, 2013.

Rabaka, Reiland. *Civil Rights Music: The Soundtracks of the Civil Rights Movement*. Lanham, MD: Lexington Books, 2016.

Robinson, Jo Ann Gibson. *The Montgomery Bus Boycott and the Women Who Started It: The Memoir of Jo Ann Gibson Robinson*. 1987; repr., Knoxville: University of Tennessee Press, 2011.

Sullivan, Patricia. *Lift Every Voice: The NAACP and the Making of the Civil Rights Movement*. New York: New Press, 2010.

Theoharis, Jeanne. *The Rebellious Life of Mrs. Rosa Parks*. 2014; rev. ed., Boston: Beacon, 2015.

Weber, Deanna Frith. "The Freedom Singers: Their History and Legacy for Music Education." PhD diss., Boston University, 2010.

Welky, David. *Marching Across the Color Line: A. Philip Randolph and Civil Rights in the World War II Era*. New York: Oxford University Press, 2014.

Wells, Peter S. *How Ancient Europeans Saw the World: Vision, Patterns, and the Shaping of the Mind in Prehistoric Times*. Princeton, NJ: Princeton University Press, 2012.

Woodward, C. Vann. *The Strange Career of Jim Crow*. 1955; rev. ed., New York: Oxford University Press, 2006.

Wynn, Neil A. *The African American Experience during World War II*. Lanham, MD: Rowman & Littlefield, 2011.

INDEX

LIST OF IMAGES

IMAGE CREDITS

Making the Movement artifact photographs on cover and throughout book: courtesy of William Davis

Front cover, 224: US Information Agency, Press and Publications Service. *Civil Rights March on Washington, D.C. [Leaders of the march leading marchers down the street.]* August 28, 1963. National Archives, https://catalog.archives.gov/id/542003

IV Stanley Wolfson, photographer. *Marchers carrying banner lead way as 15,000 parade in Harlem.* March 15, 1965. New York World-Telegram and the Sun Newspaper Photograph Collection, Library of Congress, Washington, DC, https://www.loc.gov/resource/cph.3c35695/
VIII Collection of the Smithsonian National Museum of African American History and Culture
XI Collection of the Smithsonian National Museum of African American History and Culture
XII Collection of the Smithsonian National Museum of African American History and Culture, Gift of Arthur J. "Bud" Schmidt
XIII Library of Congress Rare Book and Special Collections Division
XIV Courtesy Forest Young and Jeremy Mickel
9 Rowland Scherman. *Civil Rights March on Washington, D.C.* August 28, 1963. National Archives, https://catalog.archives.gov/id/542014

10–11, 12 Bain News Service. *National Negro Business League Executive Committee.* 1910. Bain News Service photograph collection, Library of Congress, Washington, DC, https://www.loc.gov/item/2014688320/
44–45, 46 Photographer unknown. Members of the National Association for the Advancement of Colored People. Early 1940s. Walter P. Reuther Library, Archives of Labor and Urban Affairs, Wayne State University
68–69, 70 Al Ravenna. *Holding a poster against racial bias in Mississippi are four of the most active leaders in the NAACP movement, from left: Henry L. Moon, director of public relations; Roy Wilkins, executive secretary; Herbert Hill, labor secretary, and Thurgood Marshall, special counsel.* 1956. New York World-Telegram and the Sun Newspaper Photograph Collection, Library of Congress, Washington DC, https://www.loc.gov/item/99401448/
90–91, 112 Rowland Scherman. *March on Washington for Jobs and Freedom; Photograph of a Young Woman at the Civil Rights March on Washington, D.C., with a Banner.* August 28, 1963. National Archives, https://catalog.archives.gov/id/542030
112 Warren K. Leffler. *Civil rights march on Washington, D.C.* August 28, 1963. U.S. News & World Report Magazine Photograph Collection, Library of Congress, Washington, DC, https://www.loc.gov/resource/ppmsca.03128/

142–43, 144 Warren K. Leffler. *Poor People's March at Washington Monument and Lincoln Memorial [Washington, DC].* June 19, 1968. U.S. News & World Report Magazine Photograph Collection, Library of Congress, Washington, DC, https://www.loc.gov/item/2017650272/
194 Kurt Kaiser. *Signs and posters from Black Lives Matter protests, Lafayette Park.* June 14, 2020. Wikimedia Commons, https://commons.wikimedia.org/wiki/File:Signs_and_poster_from_black_lives_matter_protests.jpg
200 Peter Pettus. *The civil rights march from Selma to Montgomery, 1965.* Library of Congress, Washington, DC, https://www.loc.gov/resource/cph.3d02329/

Published by
Princeton Architectural Press
70 West 36th Street
New York, NY 10018
www.papress.com

© 2022 David L. Crane

Printed and bound in China
25 24 23 22   4 3 2 1   First edition

ISBN 978-1-64896-108-3

Editors: Sara Stemen and Kristen Hewitt
Designers: Paul Wagner and Paula Baver

Library of Congress Control Number: 2022930790

OVERLEAF
**Roy Wilkins, A. Philip Randolph,
and Walter P. Reuther leading the
March on Washington for Jobs
and Freedom on August 28, 1963**